ALTERNATIVE G[...]

Guide to a fortnight's walking rou[...]
Tenerife, edited by Nic[...]

(6th edition)

published April 2001 by:
The Institute for Social Inventions,
20 Heber Road
London NW2 6AA
tel 020 8208 2853;
fax 020 8452 6434;
e-mail: rhino@dial.pipex.com
web: www.gomera.org.uk

© Institute for Social Inventions April 2001
Cover design: Ruth Blauert, graphic artist (offers of work to: dobedo@freenet.de)

The German map to which this guide refers (see page 9) is obtainable from the
Institute for Social Inventions for £5-85 incl. p&p

All royalties from this guide are going to the Institute for Social Inventions, an educational charity. The Institute relies on sales of publications to support its activities (see details at the end of this guide) and would be very grateful for any reviews or mentions of this booklet that give the Institute's name and address and the price: £9-99 incl. p&p

Whilst every effort has been taken to make the walk details as comprehensive as possible, you nevertheless use this guide at your own risk. Please take full note of all the safety precautions, particularly those to do with heat exhaustion. Please send in any corrections or suggestions from your travels. Update sheets for this sixth edition will be produced regularly (phone to check if there are any new ones, and then send four first class stamps to receive them). You will be credited in the sheets – and you will be sent a free copy of them. These updates are also available for free on the web (as is the first chapter of this book) via: www.gomera.org.uk

Nicholas Albery thanks all those who provided information and
assistance for this guide, particularly:
Mark Jenvey, Bob Matthews, Peggy True, John Hopkins, Spencer Lewis,
Josefine Speyer, Sara Thomas, Nicholas Saunders, Hilda and Inez, Liz
Cheno, Michael Kozdon, Hans Hubricht, Christine Holloway
Ruth Blauert and Nick Holborne.

Printed by Antony Rowe Ltd, Bumper's Farm Industrial Estate,
Chippenham, Wiltshire SN14 6LH

ISBN 0 948826 55 X

Contents Walks

Walk characteristics out of 10

	Toughness	Beauty	Hours

Introduction 3
Gomera's characteristics 3
Gomera's past 5
The walks: levels of difficulty 6
What to take 7
The best guides and map . 10
Accommodation 11
A vision for Gomera's future 12
Social experiments in Gomera 14
El Cabrito community 14
Cruz de Maria land for sale 14
Money 14
Insurance & emergencies . 15
Cheapest flights 15
Guided walks 15
Getting to Gomera 16
Ferry, hydrofoil, flights to Gomera 16
Stamps, telephone and internet 17
San Sebastian 18
Language 19
Hermigua 25
Agulo 27
Vallehermoso 30
Map overview of walks . 38
Valle Gran Rey 40
Chipude 49
Alajero 58
Imada 63
Santiago 67
Luxury hotel sauna 67
Day 7 79
Bus stop for airport 80
Two weeks on Gomera 82
Institute for Social Inventions' publications & websites 84

Day 1 Walk: San Sebastian to Hermigua 20	8	6	11
Day 2 Walk: Hermigua to Vallehermoso 27	6	8	9.5
Day 3 Walk: Vallehermoso to Chipude 32	8	9	9.5
Day 3 Alternative A: from beyond Las Hayas to Valle Gran Rey. 37	4	6	3
Day 10: Valle Gran Rey to Chipude via Cercado . 43	5	5	6
Day 3, continued, from beyond Las Hayas to Chipude 44	2	7	2
Day 3 (B): Vallehermoso to Chipude (or Valle Gran Rey) via Arure 45	6V*	9	11
Day 4: Chipude to Alajero 49	10V	10	10
Day 4 Alternative A: Chipude to Pararito, via Garajonay summit 50	6	4	2.5
Start of both the Day 4 walk and the Day 4 Alternative B walk, from Chipude to Apartadero 51	2	6	0.5
Day 4 Alternative B: half-day walk from Apartadero to Alajero 52	4	8	4
Day 4, full walk, continued, from Apartadero to Alajero 53	10V	10	9.5
Day 5: A round trip back to Alajero via Imada 60	6V	9	6
Day 5 Alternative A: Alajero to Santiago 64	5	8	7.5
The hippie beach caves/yacht marina near Santiago.. 69	1	2	1
Day 6: From Pajarito through the Parque National to El Cedro & Hermigua ... 70	7	6	7
Day 6 Alternative: Santiago to San Sebastian 74	8	5	9
Day 7 Alternative: Bar Peraza to La Laja and Lomo Fragoso or Rock Agando 80	5	6	5

*V = not for vertigo sufferers

La Gomera - An introduction

Do you fancy a week or a fortnight's break from the British winter (or summer come to that) walking around a delightfully exotic island (out in the Atlantic at the same latitude as the Spanish Sahara), with each night a cheap pension in a different village — all at a total cost, for one week, including plane, insurance, train to Gatwick, ferry, accommodation, food, drink, presents, postcards, taxis etc of about £370? If so, this booklet could be for you, since there is no other guidebook in English to the island of Gomera near Tenerife which details such a circular walking tour or which details places to stay — or which is kept so up-to-date.

If you knew of a small unspoilt paradise such as this one, would you tell all and sundry? With much hesitation I decided to do so, since future tourist development of the island is inevitable and already underway, and the more that this development can be oriented towards relatively harmless walkers staying in small pensions and people's homes, rather than towards the present plan for multi-storey hotels in tourist complexes, so much the better.

I am a lover of islands and have visited many of the Greek, Italian, French and Spanish islands of the Mediterranean, but Gomera, in the Canaries, 40 minutes by hydrofoil ferry from Tenerife, is the most beautiful and varied of them all.

Those visitors who do spend more than a day trip there are mostly young Germans, who are the world's most perceptive tourists in my opinion, but even they miss out on the island's delights. They head straight for the main tourist trap town in the West of the island, Valle Gran Rey, with its black sand beaches and juice bars and restaurants, and they rarely explore the walks outside that valley. We have walked on recognised paths for days at a time in other parts of the island without meeting any other walkers.

Gomera's characteristics

For eight of the last eleven Januaries and twice in February and once in March, I have been for a one-week walking holiday in Gomera. Gomera is the poorer traveller's substitute for Nepal, with its ravines covered with terraced farming and its mountains peeping up into the clouds — yet the walking is hardly more demanding than in the Lake District and requires no special equipment.

The island, known in Spanish as 'La Gomera', is 25 kilometres wide and 23 kilometres from North to South, and has been compared to a cake cut into a large number of pieces, with deep barrancos (ravines) between the pieces. The cause of the cake cutting was a series of volcanic explosions over the last 20 million years or so (none for the last two million years), which have left the island with a vast filled-in crater at the centre, where the climate is different to the rest of the island — here the central *cumbre* laurel forest, now a national park (the Parque Nacional de Garajonay), sometimes feels a bit like a tropical rainforest, with wet and bearded trees, often in the clouds, but exhilarating to walk through.

The variety of landscapes on Gomera is part of the island's delightfulness. You cross over the ridge from one barranco to the next and it is at times as if you had changed country. Barrancos have not only their own characteristics, but sometimes also their own weather, from the arid abandoned terraces and deserted villages of the Barranco de la Negra in the South to the thousand and one date palms of the more lush Vallehermoso ('Valley Beautiful' in English) in the North. Adding to the exotic flavour are the very sexy overendowed banana trees, the cacti with their edible red prickly pears, the groves of bamboo (or rather *Arundo donax*, a kind of cane, not really bamboo), the vineyards, and the many almond, avocado, papaya, orange trees. There are also hundreds of species of plants and trees unknown outside the Canaries.

The island is warmed by the gulf stream and cooled by the winds, with a climate that is mild the year round — often shirtsleeves weather even in January, seldom rising above 25 degrees in sum-

3

mer or sinking below 12 degrees in winter (although the weather changes fast, is sometimes too windy or very occasionally too hot for walking, is relatively cold at nights, and in the high centre of the island can be very cold and wet). The Spanish-speaking inhabitants are friendly and there are no poisonous animals or insects (although the towns can have biting flies in summer). There are fine birds and butterflies, but apart from the domestic animals – the ubiquitous dogs and goats, a few pigs, chicken, fewer still mules and donkeys, bullocks and a couple of cows and horses – there are hardly any animals at all (since I first came, the total I have glimpsed is three wild rabbits, one half-dead rat, any number of lizards and a family of wild dogs. On several trips a dog seems to have got very attached to us and has wanted to follow us for days. It might be kind to shoo such dogs away at an early stage if you do not intend to provide for them – your pension will almost certainly not welcome them). In 2000, six giant 18in lizards (four females and two males of the species Gallotia gomerana) believed to have been extinct for 500 years were found in the cliffs of Valle Gran Rey, were taken to the University of La Laguna in Tenerife for study and were later replaced in a safer and unreported location.

Re this relative lack of wildlife in the Canaries, see *Fauna de las Islas Canarias* by Jose Manuel Moreno, Ediciones Turquesa, 1992, ISBN 84 604 3599 7, available from the Visitor's Centre on La Gomera, or from bookshops on the island. The Canaries have no foxes, deer, badgers, hares – and hedgehogs only because they have been introduced to some of the islands (but not La Gomera). There are seven species of bats (but only four so far have been spotted in La Gomera), none of which seem to have been introduced. All the other mammals have been introduced: rabbits, three sorts of rat, a wild goat from North Africa and what seems top be a ground squirrel (Atlantoxerus getulus) also from North Africa. There are also sea mammals: dolphins (Delphinus delphus and Tursiops truncatus) and whales (Physeter macrocephalus and Globicephala macrorhynchus) and something called in Spanish Zifo comun (Ziphius cavirostris).

Of birds of prey, the most common are the kestrel – in La Gomera, an endemic sub-species, Flaco tinnunculus canariensis, and the common buzzard (Buteo buteo). There are also sparrowhawks and a few ospreys and even fewer peregrine falcons.

The large birds that fly out from rocky paths with a whirr from their wings are likely to be partridges (Alectoris barbara koenigi) – often in pairs.

The best time to go walking there (and often the cheapest time for airplane tickets, and the time when you can most easily find accommodation in the pensions) is when it is both cool and out of peak season – for instance in January (it is fun to be there for the big Three Kings' Festival on January 5th, when the children give their present requests to the passing floats). February is lovely with the wild flowers. February is ideal – there is less chance of storms and very windy weather than in January. By March it is already getting a little too sunny by the middle of the day.

You can check the next few days' weather forecast for the Canaries (or at least for Tenerife) without charge on your TV's teletext (BBC1 Ceefax Page 410) or on the Internet (for instance the weather section at www.bbc.co.uk/weather/); or at 50p a minute by phoning Metcall International on 0336 411 211 using a touchtone phone (when you get through, press 5, when asked, then 194 for the Canaries).

The language of Gomera nowadays is Spanish. Some of the older inhabitants can still use the intriguing Gomeran whistling language, 'el silbo', useful for conveying quite detailed information from mountain-top to mountain-top, such as 'meet you in the cafe by the plaza for a drink at 12'. Some whistlers can make themselves understood up to five miles away, with a following wind, it is claimed. The whistle is demonstrated at some of the tourist restaurants, is recognised by

UNESCO as a language whose survival is threatened, and is taught to 9 and 10 year olds in specialised classes in school. The whistle compresses all spoken sounds to four consonants and two vowels, using varying tone and length. Some experts say that the whistling originated from the Berbers in the high Atlas in Morocco, although the Turks near the Black Sea in the Kuskoy valley do a similar form of whistling.

A good German booklet with colour photos and Latin and Spanish names for about hundred specimens of the island's flora is *Planzenführer Kanärische Inseln* by Andrea and Thomas Müller, available from the craft shop in Hermigua and from various shops on the island and perhaps from a German bookshop on the web. Or a similar number of specimens are covered in less detail, with their English and Latin names (not their Spanish) in *La Gomera Plants and Flowers Guide* (two folding posters) available for a £2 cheque from Discovery Walking Guides, 10 Tennyson Close, Northampton NN5 7HJ. For a website with a few photos of plants to be found in La Gomera and a long list of Latin and English names for flowers and fruit trees (and other interesting material about Gomera), see http://home.eunet.no/~jorgenaa/travel/gomera/efrukt.html

Gomera's past

The generally accepted theory is that the Canary islands arose through volcanic explosions from the sea. Some scholars, however, believe that Gomera and the Canaries may at one time have been connected to the African mainland. The island's original Guanche inhabitants were mainly very tall, sturdy and with blue eyes and fair hair, although intermixed with various shipwrecked others. The Guanche may have had Berber connections (in Tenerife, 'Guan' meant 'man', but each island had its own language, with similarities between the islands. The languages are now lost, although some Guanche surnames and place names and about 3000 words survive). The Guanche buried the mummified bodies of their dead in bricked-up caves in as inaccessible spots as possible, and they followed a Stone Age way of life (without even the use of the potter's wheel) into the middle ages. They had no bread, using a *gofio* barley flour instead. They had no chisels or metal instruments. Supposedly their only way of fishing was to jump into the sea so as to frighten the fish into their reed nets. On Tenerife island even the art of swimming is said to have been unknown. None of the Canary Islands except Hierro discovered how to produce alcohol by distillation, so that water and palm juice were the only drinks. They had no cotton or flax, only chamois leather. And no needles, only awls made of fish bone or palm thorns. They used cattle as a symbol of wealth, and the nobility had slaves or commoners as servants. Shields were made from the bark of the dragon tree.

There are many theories as to the origins of these people – the fact that only Peruvians, Guanche and Egyptians mummify their corpses perhaps argues for a common origin for these peoples, with one theory being that civilization spread from the Canaries to Egypt rather than the other way around. (The Guanche method of mummifying a body was to remove the entrails, to wash the body in cold water mixed with salt twice a day, to rub it with grease, resins and lards, and to expose it to the sun for a fortnight.)

The land is fertile, producing, inter alia, bananas, mangoes, dates, guavas, apricots, potatoes and barley. There are only 69 rainy days a year, and these are normally only intermittently so, often with another part of the island still rain-free, there is no dampness at night nor even at sunrise or sunset. There is no winter.

It is hardly surprising that in classical times the Canary Islands were associated with Elysium and the Garden of Hesperides and with the remains of a lost Atlantis, and they were dubbed 'The Fortunate Isles'.

At least on Gran Canaria, polyandry was practised, with a woman often married to three husbands, who enjoyed their marital rights in monthly rotation. Divorce was normally without rancour and by mutual agreement. Guanche kings listened to plaintiffs under dragon trees, which is also where the princesses danced. (Dragon trees are of the lily family, a sort of asparagus or spurge. There is only one dragon tree in Gomera – see route 46 North of Alajero on the German map.) Guanche people were generous and friendly if not provoked but 'capable of terrible reprisals if attacked'.

Inevitably these islands attracted visitors. There were Arab visitors (from the 10th century onwards), a Genoese expedition (1291) and a Portuguese one in 1341 which reported to King Alfonso IV about Gomera's 'good number of streams and deliciously tasty pigeons, which feed on laurel berries and cherries'. Most of the Canary Islands were conquered for the crown of Castille in the 15th century by Juan de Bethencourt, a Norman nobleman, but he was unable to subdue Gomera, which did not become part of the Spanish crown until 1488; and, even then, it was as much through contact and trade as through armed conquest. 1488, however, was the date of a Spanish atrocity in Gomera. Herman Peraza, of Andalusian ancestry, was assassinated by Gomerans whilst carrying on an affair with Yballa, a young Gomeran woman. Peraza's widow, Dona Beatriz de Bobadilla, took refuge in the San Sebastian tower (which still looks very defensible in San Sebastian – it is worth a visit, in the hinterland behind the far end of the beach). She sought help from another Andalusian nobleman, Pedro de Vera, who came with 400 veteran soldiers and executed Guanche captives, some by chopping off their hands and feet, some by hanging, some by dragging with horses. Captured Guanche children became slaves.

In 1492, Gomera and the neighbouring smaller Hierro islands were the last landfalls for Columbus on his voyage towards America. Gomera defended itself successfully when besieged by the British fleet under Admiral Charles Windham in 1743 (see the triumphalist mural in the church of San Sebastian). The Canaries were involved in the Spanish Civil War, with the rich tending to side with the fascists, but they shared Spain's neutrality in the Second World War. To this day some Gomerans hanker for their island's independence from Spain, as the occasional lively wall graffiti bear testimony. Local people all seem to talk of the politicians presently in power as being corrupt and unimpressive.

Gomera was badly hit by the demise of the cochineal industry (red dyes processed from female scale insect bugs living on the prickly pear cacti which were imported from Mexico for the purpose. These dyes have now been largely replaced by aniline ones). There has been an attempt to develop banana plantations as an alternative. The bananas are rather on the small size for the world market, but are mainly bought up by Spain. There are several closed tuna factories in the South West of the island, abandoned because of over-fishing. The population of Gomera has fallen from a peak of 30,000 to just under 17,000 today (it is stable at this level). Many have left to look for work in Spain, Britain and Venezuela.

For further details on the history of Gomera, see 'The Canary Islands' by Salvadoz Lopez Herrera, ISBN 84 400 4705 3.

The walks: levels of difficulty

The walks in this booklet vary from an all-day marathon with constant uphills and downhills through steep barrancos (Day 4), to an easy seven hour walk which is for the first part a stroll downhill along wide and gently undulating paths (Day 6). There is one walk (Day 3) which involves twenty metres of fairly easy scrambling up a rockface. You need, in other words, to be generally fit, able to walk an average of 18 (up to 28 kilometres) each day, uphill and downhill, and to be of a relatively adventurous and independent disposition. However, for each of the walks an easier and shorter alternative is also detailed.

I love the feeling of walking off into the mountains

on an epic adventure within 24 hours of leaving London, but Bob, my walking companion one year, says that he thinks most people would prefer to acclimatise more gradually, to have a day or two's rest before starting walking, or do only the shorter versions of the walks to begin with. The main suggested walk on Day 1 is a long one. For readers who share Bob's persuasion, the best solution might be either to do a shorter version of the Day 1 walk (either just the shorter first part or the longer second part) or to take a bus at mid-day on the first day in Gomera to Alajero, and book into the pension there for a couple of nights (phoning first to make sure there is room), and to start off with the very easy first part of the mainly-downhill Day 6 walk (probably leaving out the after-lunch uphill slog) and then the easy and very beautiful Day 5 Alternative A walk (Alajero to Santiago, perhaps thumbing a lift once you get to the tarmac road).

For those who have time to do only one walk in this guide, my recommendation is the Day 5 one to Imada. My favourite walk in this guide is, however, the Day 4 one, but this is truly a long and arduous walk with many barrancos, and many readers may prefer the shorter alternatives that are suggested for that day.

There are enough alternative walks in this book for a second circuit of the island. See the section at the end of this guide for a suggested second week of walks.

When you walk on the old tracks of Gomera, you are using the road and path systems of the pre-industrial, pre-automobile age. The largest old paths are only about three metres wide and the smallest less than one metre wide, along with steep steps cut into barranco sides.

In the mountains, some find that a long stick (for instance 8 to 10 ft of bamboo) is useful for reducing jarring of the knees and for moving fast and keeping balance better – you sometimes see local people using one to leap their way downhill. There is a bamboo grove you come to on the Day 1 walk in this guide.

I have described each of the walks in enormous detail. For UK walks this can be unnecessary, as the Ordnance Survey maps are reliable and there are often houses or people within range that you can consult if you get lost. In Gomera, you could be days on some of these walks without someone else coming upon you, and often the routes are in the middle of nowhere or the nearest hamlet has long since been abandoned. Furthermore, the maps are unreliable and the sides of some of the barrancos are so precipitous that there is only one way down and you have to know where to find it. From years of experience of using other Gomera guides, I know that the details they give tend to be inadequate, and that one can end up tired and bad-tempered and even dangerously lost late in the evening. My aim has been to provide enough details so that, for example, if you come to a house where you are supposed to take a fork, the house is described sufficiently for you to know which one it is, or, if the house has since changed its appearance, that there should be enough other details and compass directions to keep you on the right path. Nevertheless, because so much detail will most of the time not be needed, and is there to refer to only if you get confused, I have put the principal directions in italics. For the most part, these will be sufficient on their own.

The timings given for these walks are very slow, and allow for breaks and even for getting lost occasionally (despite being relatively unfit, born 1948, with a desk-bound job and having to stop all the time to write notes, I tend to knock a third off the times in this book). Very fast walkers may be able to do these walks in half the time specified. But then, what would be the point of rushing through so much beauty?

What to take

What you take with you depends on the degree of risk with which you feel comfortable. I have an extreme aversion to walking up and down steep ravines in the heat encumbered with a rucksack, so normally all I take with me for the week are the following – and note that one reasonably cheap place for walking and camping equipment is Tarpaulin & Tent Ltd, PO Box 350, Esher, KT10 8DZ (credit card orders, tel 020 8873 3797); other mail order places include CRM (tel 0800 413635; www.crm mailorder.co.uk), Bourne Sports (tel 01782 410411), Complete Outdoors (tel 01442 873133; www.complete-outdoors.co.uk) and Field and Trek (tel 01268 494444; www.fieldandtrek.co.uk).

• A bag small and light enough to fit in the plane's overhead locker, so that I don't have to wait for the luggage to reach the carousels (some airlines insist on less than 5kg in weight). In this bag I put a book for the plane and a change of clothes for the return journey and some anti-mosquito cream for the first night in San Sebastian (the only place I have ever been bothered by mosquitoes). I then leave the bag in San Sebastian, either at a pension, if they are willing, or otherwise with the car hire firm in Calle del Medio, who kindly put it under their table (I give them a 500 pesetas tip at the end for their trouble).

• A pair of corduroy trousers (not only for warmth but to protect my legs against brambles, cacti and sun).

• A light and somewhat shower-resistant woollen zip-up 'fleece' jacket with interior pockets (to which I sew on Velcro sticky strips to keep them closed) and exterior zipped pockets (available in most sport shops for about £25. This on warm days I carry tied by the arms round my waist or neck. It is for the occasional cold and windy times.

• A windproof sunhat with a broad rim called the Norfolk Intrepid. An expensive luxury at £29-95 (inc. p&p) but it does stay on, with a double shoelace under the chin and to the back of the head. It is made of strong cotton and can be folded up. Available by phone and credit card from Norfolk Headwear (tel 0845 602 0231). I see that CRM (tel 0800 413635) advertise a Unisex Explorer Hat for £19.40 (inc. p&p) but this has just a one cord to hold it on.

One woman I met suffered so badly from heat exhaustion from having no hat and from running out of water, on a short walk towards Alajero, that she begged her boyfriend to leave her to die. She survived. But beware.

• A long-sleeved safari-type shirt, with lots of button-down pockets, which I wear over a T-shirt.

• In 2000, I took also a Domke PhoTogs sleeveless, ventilated jacket, designed for photographers on expeditions, with about 18 pockets (available from a variety of sites on the web if you do a search – the cheapest at present is www.fargo-ent.com who charge $59.97, postage extra); this is not an essential item and is slightly hot and heavy, but it meant I could carry more items than normal, and still remain without a rucksack.

In this multitude of pockets, or in my money pouch, I carry:

• Passport and tickets and money.

• Dental tape, a miniature travelling toothbrush and toothpaste.

• A few strips of elastoplast (in case of blisters as much as for anything else). If you are susceptible to blisters, you might ask your chemist shop for the Scholl plasters for blisters, lined with hydrocolloid gel, or any similar type.

• Two thin pairs of socks and a change of underpants.

• An ordinary half litre plastic bottle of mineral water. I refill it with tapwater or streams on the island – the Gomeran water tastes fine.

In an emergency, you could get nourishment and some liquid by eating the red fruit of the universally-found prickly pear cactus. But as I and my friends have found, although the fruit looks enticingly unprickly, it has very many tiny thorns which can easily get embedded in your hands and lips. Use some form of glove when opening it up.

• A bar of chocolate and a piece of cheese – for lunch and emergency rations. The food and the water I put in a little bum bag round my stomach.

• A small tin of atrixo hand cream.

• A small tube of factor 15 suncream. Even though I was covered with clothes and a hat from head to toe during my March visit, the back

of my hands got painfully sunburnt.
- Some aspirins just in case.
- A disposable razor.
- Some folded paper kitchen towels.
- A compass with a swivelling rim marked with degrees, for more accurate comparison of forks and turn-offs on the map with exterior reality. (I tend to give the directions roughly as say SSW and then more accurately in degrees, say 195 degrees.)
- The German map detailed below, which, with this guide, I put in an A4-sized plastic map holder (from a camping shop), which attaches with a cord round the neck. With a string I attach my compass to this map holder.
- A biro and small notebook with a needle secured in the cover, ready threaded with several feet of thread wound around the cover. There is always something that needs mending within the week.
- A small plastic whistle (about £1 from a camping shop) to call for assistance if needed, or to identify one's whereabouts to one's companions (the sound of a whistle carries further than shouting. The quite useful code we devised was for 3 long whistles to mean 'come here', 2 long whistles to mean 'I'm coming' and 1 long whistle to mean 'I hear you' or 'this is where I am'. Recognised internationally to mean 'help!' are either 6 long whistles repeated at intervals or 3 short, 3 long, 3 short – SOS in morse code).
- A very small torch (camping shops sell a 10cm plastic torch using one AA battery for about £2).
- Being thin and susceptible to the cold, I also take a pair of long-johns and a cashmere sweater. I tend to tie the sweater to my waist and put the long-johns in my Domke jacket. But for those who prefer it, a small rucksack could fit these kinds of items.
- If the five-day forecast mentions rain I take a lightweight poncho mac (costing less than £10).

My own more eccentric extras include:
- Vitamin C. American medical researchers have found that those who take 1,000 mg of Vitamin C three times a day for three days before they start exercising, and, for seven days afterwards, will dramatically cut the crippling soreness of stiff muscles.
- 2 wax earplugs. In the villages, the cocks start crowing at 5am or earlier. Alajero can be the most cacophonous place on the island, with competing cocks, howling dogs and a clock tower with its own loudhailer giving a synthesised imitation of Big Ben each hour.
- A sheet of A4 paper with many poems reduced onto two sides of paper for learning by heart and one of those miniature penguin books for reading matter.

For those who really do not mind going up and down ravines all day in the sun with a heavy pack on their back (you will! you will! By the end of the first day you will regret every unnecessary ounce of weight. Bob resisted all my sneering in London and insisted on coming with a pack weighing 3.5 kg. He dumped as much of it as he could after the first couple of days of walking), the ultimate protection against pensions being full or against getting caught on a cold mountain for the night, would be to take a tent and sleeping bag. You may camp in Gomera on any terrace or piece of land that is 50 metres or more from a house, as long as it is not within the Parque Nacional boundaries and as long as you light no fires. (There are certain places in the park where you can camp if you have a permit – the park offices are Icona, Carretera General del Sur 20, San Sebastian, tel 922 870105.)

Back-packers could include other luxuries such as a towel. In Gomeran pensions, on the occasions where towels are not supplied, I use my bed sheet for a towel in the morning.

A luxury for a group walking together might be to book their pensions the day before by phone, where possible, and then to send their heavy luggage ahead of them by taxi, but you would need good Spanish and compliant taxi drivers and pensions.

A safeguard would be to have or to rent a mobile phone which works in the Canaries. We have found that a mobile phone functions

OK on walks near to San Sebastian, but not in the deeper barrancos near Chipude and Alojera, nor on the Day 6 walk through the central forest.

Another safeguard is to take travelling companions (or to join up with other walkers once there – you might have to go to Valle Gran Rey to have the best chance of finding them). I think four is the ideal number – any more and you may have difficulty finding rooms for the night in the smaller villages. With four people, if one person is injured, a friend can stay with them whilst two others go for help. But my wife and I have walked happily in Gomera as a pair, and I have enjoyed solo walks, and have met several solo travellers, the most intrepid being a British retired coal miner of 65 who was running 20km a day over the mountains with a pack on his back, and who came running up to us when we were lost in the clouds. He was like an angel of mercy, redirecting us on our way.

A final safety precaution is always to remember to look out for your onward path in the distance, often on the other side of a barranco. Sometimes the way in to a path can be clearly seen from afar but is very hard to find once right on top of it.

The first year I went in gym shoes with an insole, which were fine as it so happened, but it is probably better to have a pair of very lightweight boots which do not slip on rocks, and which, from long previous experience, do not give you blisters and which have plenty of bounce in the soles. You shouldn't need to pay more than £15 for a good pair of boots from a chain such as Shoefayre (tel 020 8951 4028). I add a bouncy insole.

The best guides map & websites

The almost essential companion to this guide is the widely used German-published Gomera walking map with the green and yellow cover. This last is entitled 'La Gomera, Wanderrouten-Übersicht', published by Goldstadt-verlag (Herr Schäfer and colleagues, Finkenstein Strasse 6, 75179 Pforzheim, Germany, tel 00 49 7231 94470) or available from the Institute for Social Inventions for £5·85 inc. p&p (20 Heber Road, London NW2 6AA; credit card orders to 020 8208 2853). The walks in this present booklet assume that you have this map and refer to its numbering of routes. The old edition is widely available from kiosks and bookshops on the island.

The map is particularly helpful in clearly distinguishing asphalted roads from unpaved roads, and both from footpaths, whilst mountain ranges are shaded in, which is easier to grasp visually than the contour lines that are also included. Most of the other Gomeran maps on sale are to be avoided, as they are far less detailed and less up-to-date, and contain more errors (although there is a newish 1 in 35,000 scale German map, which looks OK if short on detail, but it does not follow the walk numbering given in this guide).

For those planning to stay on Gomera for more than a fortnight, or to walk on Tenerife too, it would be worth consulting not only this present guide and the above map, but the excellent guide I used myself on earlier visits, 'Landscapes of Southern Tenerife and La Gomera' by Noel Rochford, published in 1988 by Sunflower Books (£8·99 – and for an update on the guide send 50p and an SAE to Sunflower Books Update Service, 12 Kendrick Mews, London SW7 3HG, tel 020 7589 1862). My only quibbles with this guide are that it does not give places to stay, or even which villages have places to stay; it assumes you are staying in fixed places rather than taking a circular tour; it says you can follow its walks in reverse if necessary, although I have got hopelessly lost when trying to; its walks are not detailed enough – we got lost very often; its maps look authoritative but seem slightly less so in practice – nor are they related to the 57 walks in the map now used by all walkers (and referred to above).

A very basic and not very useful Lonely Planet guide to the Canaries as a whole is available and a Rough guide is in preparation. Two other walk books seem of limited usefulness, confusing to try to use and already out of date: *La Gomera for Walkers* and *Walk! La Gomera*. The latter has a map that can be ordered, entitled La Gomera, at a scale of 1 in 40,000.

The most widely available walking books for Gomera are in German and are relatively thorough. If you can read German, the best of the bunch for walkers, although out of date, is 'Kanarische Wanderungen auf La Gomera, El Hierro und La Palma' by Ursula and Adam Reifenberger, published by Wander Handbuch at 22DM (Conrad Stein Verlag, Andreas-Gayk-Str. 7-111, D 2300 Kiel 1, Germany, tel 00 49 431 93377). There is also a German guide based on the German map that I recommended above – it is called 'La Gomera', published 1993 by the map's publishers Goldstadverlag (address above). This guide too is not detailed enough. I met one walker who said she kept wanting to throw it down the ravine in frustration.

Two fairly useful websites, both offering general information on Gomera are: www.gomera.net (which also has ferry times and various apartments) and www.timah.net (which offers hiking tours, mainly for German speakers).

There is a German Gomeran tourist newspaper called Der Valle-Bote, (tel 922 805759; www.gomeranews.com) which contains useful local news, information and small ads.

Accommodation

Gomera is fairly short of pensions and apartments.

Though less true in the last year or two, visiting Valle Gran Rey in particular, the main tourist town, used to involve a desperate scramble for rooms – a friend and I once discussed buying a ship as a floating hotel for the port there. Landlords in Valle Gran Rey will often only want to rent you a place if you are staying for a week (it is worth asking tourists for spare space in their apartments). In other places such as Alajero, there seems to be only one small pension, and, if that's full, you have to either find somebody to put you up, or get a lift to the next town.

There are many villages marked with big black dots on Gomeran maps which look substantial, but which in fact do not have places to stay. It is worth knowing which do and which do not. For the record (and please let me know if you discover other places, or indeed any other information about Gomera worth including in update and correction sheets), the only places I know of with rooms or houses ('casas') for rent are as follows (those places with more or less adequate availability are in bold, and I am listing the places in my rough order of preference, for their beauty and general delightfulness – and that of their surrounding countryside; further details of actual accommodation in these places can be found further on in this guide):

Alajero (a new hotel is also under construction here)

Agulo

Benchijigua (renovated houses rentable from the Fred Olsen/Jardin Tecina people on 922 895125 or 922 895205)

Chipude

Tagaluche

Vallehermoso

Las Hayas (Bar Montaña has two rooms only, a single room for 3,500 pesetas, a double room for 4,000 pesetas)

Alojera (apartments by the beach there, speak to Miguel in the fish restaurant; also Casas Ossorio, tel 922 800334, apartments for 2 to 4 people)

Arure

El Cedro (La Cabana, an 'alternative pension' run by a German couple, Peter Barth and Anna Kienitz, tel 922 880318, due to re-open in May 2001. They grow herbal teas and are using solar power. There is also a camping site, at 300 pesetas per person per night, run by the La Vista restaurant, tel 922 880944. The latter can also supply information on a house for rent there, El Refugio)

Epina (Casa Rural Epina, tel 922 800000)

La Dama

Hermigua

San Sebastian

Santiago

Valle Gran Rey

Most pensions cost from 2,500 to 4,500 pesetas a night (if staying for one night only) for two people. In Valle

Gran Rey you are likely to be charged nearer to 5,000, and in San Sebastian 4,000. If you are overcharged by a pension (or a restaurant) ask for their Hoja de Reclamaciones book. I have never had occasion to do this, but one reader wrote that it produced magical results ('if they have three substantiated complaints, their establishment can be threatened with closure'). Or you can send a complaint in English or Spanish to: Direccion Territorial del Turismo, Caseria de la Presidencia y Turismo, Calle Marina 57, Santa Cruz, Tenerife 38001 (tel 922 244245), enclosing receipts if you have them. You may wish to copy your complaint to the Instituto Nacio-nal de Consumo, Calle Principe de Vergasa 54, Madrid 28006.

In some guide books, it suggests phoning in advance to reserve a place in a pension. We do so on occasion, but the owners have not always been willing to take one night bookings over the phone (they are more likely to say yes, they have a place, if they see you in the flesh, once you have hung around for long enough for them to see that you are not some wild animal). Only near Easter, have we ever yet run into trouble by just turning up in the early evening. However, even this small guide may help aggravate the situation, at least in the short term, before new pensions spring up to meet the demand. And it might be worth phoning the only pension in the town of Alajero well before arriving there (see the Day 4 walk below) – also the only pension in Chipude (see the Day 3 walk below).

When arriving in a new place, the simplest way to find a pension, if the ones in this booklet are unavailable, is to ask for tips from other travellers, or to ask the shops or bar tenders, or to knock on the doors of the larger houses. (Bar tenders, by the way, sometimes get commissions from taxi drivers to phone their taxis for you, which is then added to your taxi bill. I imagine that the same applies to bars which phone up pensions for you.)

Use water sparingly in pensions. The island has been through years of water shortage.

For those determined to stay in one place throughout their holiday, my recommendation would be a balcony room or apartment for about 4000 pesetas for two people per night in the lovely Pension Villaverde in Alojera (tel 922 895162), my favourite town on the island. You can pick oranges from the balcony and there are a number of superb day walks within easy reach. Otherwise Liz and John Bicheno of **Casas Canarias** (Apartamentos Bellvista, Laguna Santiago, Santiago, Gomera, tel Gomera 922 895570 w or 922 895557 h; tel London 020 7485 4387) rent out some 15 houses or apartments – for instance, at the cheaper end, £252 for one week for two people in El Cabezo (near Benchijigua) or £385 for three bedrooms (in the upper part of Hermi-gua). They can possibly also help you find a house to buy in La Gomera. Likewise, **Casas Las Hayas** (tel 922 804 077, web: www.canary-islands.com/uk/gom-cr.html) have houses in La Gomera to rent – for instance, three houses in Las Hayas (overlooking the Valle Gran Rey barranco) sleeping from two to eight people (the 2 person house costs 6800 a night). Or try the **Centre de Iniciativas y Turismo Rural** (for the North of the island), Callejon de Ordaiz, 38820 Hermigua (tel 9322 144101; gomera @canary-islands.com; www.canary-islands.com).

A vision for Gomera's future

If only more of the millions of pesetas being poured into the island by the European Community could be spent, not on prestige projects such as the underused inter-island airport near Santiago (started in 1964, finally completed in 1999, but slower for tourists to use than the hydrofoil ferry) or on asphalting yet more roads, but rather on small 'intermediate development' projects of more long-term benefit to local people, or for the encouragement of small-scale tourism. Desirable ways to spend this money include: tax breaks and subsidies for local people opening pensions, repair of the water aqueducts, subsidised rehousing in the derelict villages, a small hospital in Valle Gran Rey, training local people as walk guides, marking the footpaths more thoroughly with marker dots (this is beginning to happen), clearing brambles, bushes, fallen trees and rocks from the most impeded footpaths (without over-'improving' them, as has happened in the Parque Nacional, which takes away their character), improving the island's rubbish dumps, removing sewer outlets from the Valle Gran Rey beaches, even collecting all the wrecked cars that litter the island's roads. It might even be worth printing a basic tourist training leaflet for local pensions and for restaurants which want to attract tourists, explaining, for instance, that although local people are hardy and may like the restaurant's front doors open all night, the average foreigners may appreciate more warmth – and that pensions may like to supply more than one blanket per bed.

My best vision for Gomera's future is that it could go in the direction of Skyros island in Greece, where one restauranteur gathered together all the businesses on the island into an association that successfully helped fight off the development of huge package holiday hotels. Another far-sighted political move would be the bringing in of planning controls to rule out any pensions or hotels of more than two storeys or for more than twenty guests. In Skyros, visitors stay in the rooms of local people's homes – this way the money goes straight to the inhabitants rather than to some foreign hotel chain, and the development of a uniform package holiday experience is discouraged. God forbid that the nightmare development of Tenerife should spread throughout Gomera.

The signs are not good though, with another large hotel (for near La Dama) planned by the Fred Olsen Hotel Tecina people.

Gomera needs development to renovate the ghost villages and abandoned houses and terraced farming, and to prevent further depopulation. This will happen anyway. Land in Gomera is already shooting up in value, and will continue to do so, with perhaps a brief lull as the euro puts an end to untaxed money from Germany. One factor pointing in the direction of higher prices is the development of satellite phones and solar-powered computers, which mean that many self-employed and business people can work in rural areas, however remote. Island paradises such as Gomera within range of cheap flights will become very sought after.

More and more Germans are also likely to buy land in Gomera. They risk eventually squeezing out local people, since foreigners pay far over the local price. In 1997 I saw an isolated not-very-attractive house in El Cedro (a hamlet in a picturesque barranco on the fringes of the rainforest near Hermigua in the NW) advertised in a Tenerife estate agency as 3 bedrooms with 6,000 sq metres of land, at the very high price of 26,250,000 pesetas (£128,000) – and still for sale in 2000. Local people would normally pay between 2 and 3 million pesetas for a house and garden, plus between 1,000 and 1,500 pesetas per square metre for extra land, a likely total in this case of under 10 million pesetas.

Despite this, I would love to be involved in a project to purchase and renovate one of the ghost villages in Gomera in a sensitive way (my favourite such village was La Manteca and the houses in the barranco below it, just SE of El Drago, but I may have missed my chance – a couple of houses there have now already been renovated. See my account of it in the Day 4 walk below. Another beautiful empty hamlet is the one at El Azadoe near Imada – see the Day 6 Alternative walk below – although this only has donkey path access).

Incidentally, Gomera, though officially administered by Tenerife, has its own governing cabinet (Sr. Casimiro Curbelo Curbelo, c/ Real 31, 38.800 San Sebastian, Gomera, Excmo. Cabildo Insular De La Gomera).

Social experiments in Gomera
El Cabrito community

I have come across several interesting social experiments on my walks that have been started primarily with German-speaking travellers in mind. The first and most inaccessible one, I stumbled on when walking from San Sebastian to Santiago along the coast. The Austrian free-sex and emotional-self-expression therapy commune, run by happenings artist Otto Mühl, bought the whole bay of El Cabrito as an arts centre. No road leads to the hamlet, so access is by sea or by footpaths. Otto Mühl is out of jail now and living with the extreme communards in Portugal (he was given seven years' jail sentence in Austria for heroin offences and for making love to a fourteen year old). However, the rest of the commune has now broken free from his leadership and has become very respectable. They run their own motorboat which may be able to include you on their run to town, if you happen to be there at the right times. They cultivate bananas and other crops. And they offer painting courses and holidays of at least a week. All their guests tend to be Austrian or German, but they say that they are open to other nationalities. For further details see the Day 6 Alternative walk from Santiago to San Sebastian.

Cruz de Maria land for sale

Another social experiment, called Cruz de María, was offering land on 99 year leases at 5,000 DM (about £2000) for tiny plots of about 50 square metres. 20 plots were sold, mainly to young Germans who would camp on site whilst building their drystone wall houses. The site was two kilometres SW of Alajero towards Quise (take the unpaved track out of town that heads SW from the South Western corner of the football pitch, towards the chapel on the far hill, and follow the main car track where it forks right in a hundred metres; about five minutes after this first fork, fork left, continuing downhill). When I last visited, the community was not the couple of newly built houses that you come to on the left hand side, or the caravans on the left hand side, but rather the site opposite the caravans, with a car track bulldozed up through the site. The site was a bare hillside with a few palm trees and abandoned terraces, overlooking the sea and the island of Hierro in the distance. The scheme is the dreamchild of Uwe Klein-Schmidt. Only a kitchen and a shower area with a bamboo screen had been erected on site, but there were grandiose plans for a theatre, bath house, cafe, hotel and bus (this last to be shared with the inhabitants of Alajero). However, the last I heard was that all but four of the 20 people who have paid for their plots want their money back, and some have gone to court in Gomera to try to obtain it. The Guardia Civil turned up on site to prevent further building or camping, as Uwe did not have planing permission. But Uwe is now said to have planning permission, and to be wanting to build three houses for sale, so as to make money for his more ambitious plans (Cruz de María, c/o Uwe Klein-schmidt, Reutber-Gerstr. 9, 8000 München 70, Germany, tel 00 49 89 76 4315; fax 00 49 89 72 12753).

Money

Canary Island money-change places seem to offer a considerably worse rate than at Gatwick. But nowadays, if you should need them, there are a number of street machines on Gomera offering cash from your cards (in Valle Gran Rey, Vallehermoso, Agulo, Hermigua and San Sebastian). For a week, I always take a reserve of £100 in travellers cheques, some English currency and £250 in Spanish pesetas. This last is normally about £40 more in pesetas than I end up spending (and I eat and drink with no eye on the price – my companions tend to spend only £180 in a week). I club together with my companions and change my money at the 24-hour Travelex bureau in Gatwick airport. We pay £2-50 for their buy-back service, so that on our return they will buy back unspent pesetas at the price we paid and without commission.

Insurance and emergencies

The cheapest travel insurance I could find when last needing to renew seemed to be Primary Direct Travel Insurance (tel 0890 444 3434) who charge £12·78 for 10 days (we pay them £87·78 as a couple for one year worldwide). Choice magazine recommends as being even cheaper Berry, Birch and Noble (£10-50 for ten days, tel 0800 854 074) or Screentrade (£10-50 at www.screentrade.co.uk).

If you run into severe problems, the British consul is at Plaza Weyler 8, Santa Cruz de Tenerife (tel 922 28 68 63).

To contact an operator you dial 003; to contact an English-speaking operator your dial 025; for the emergency services you dial 062 for the police or 112 for a medical problem.

In San Sebastian, the police phone number is 922 870062. The hospital is 922 870440. The ambulance is 922 870203.

Cheapest flights

For a cheap flight, try one of the travel companies listed on the web or in media such as Time Out, the Evening Standard or Teletext. Because I often do not have the time to shop around, I tend to use Thomas Cook Direct for flight-only bookings (tel 0870 566 6222), who offer fairly keen prices. In 2001, however, I used Club Travel (tel 0161 968 2005) paying them £149 for a return daytime flight to Tenerife in February (a Monarch charter flight). They actually got the tickets from Avro (tel 020 8695 4321) so you may like to try going direct to them. Occasionally, we have been able to get standby prices nearer the time as low as £56 return. Try, for instance, an Internet bargain flight bookings service that is linked in with most of the major operators (www.bargainholidays.co.uk; or phone their hotline on 01222 555 656). Or a less informative cheap flights Internet site (at: www.cheapflights.co.uk/Tenerife.html) which gives you relevant travel agency numbers and web addresses and specimen flight quotes. The only other web sites I could find that gave swift and useful results were: www.netflights.com and www.ebookers.com

For safety's sake, if it is your first visit to Gomera, it might be worth booking a flight around the time of the full moon, so that if you get lost in the barrancos at night, you have more chance of finding your way out.

Guided walks

At least four companies are now offering guided walking holidays in Gomera: Explore Worldwide (tel 01252 333031) charge £645 incl. flights for 15 days in Tenerife, Gomera (a circular walk series round the island) and Hierro (we met their group of 15 in 2001, six of whom were retired; they were finding the walks hard, although they were doing easy, short walks relative to those in this guide). Waymark (tel 01753 516477) charge from £440 to £515 incl. flights for 7 nights in Gomera. Then there is the interesting: Sherpa Expeditions of 131A Heston Road, Hounslow, Middlesex TW5 0RD (tel 020 8569 6627; www.sherpa-walking-holidays.co.uk). Perhaps inspired by this present guidebook, they offer circular walks around the island, staying at different pensions, with flight, insurance and most meals included for about £655. The walkers are normally couples, and are given a few sheets of paper detailing the suggested walks (sometimes modified and easier versions of those in this guide) and tokens for their pensions and meals. They are then left to get on with it, but with their bags taken for them by the local representatives. The local agents on Gomera for all three of these firms (and for Casas Canarias mentioned in the 'Accommodation' section above) will normally be John and Liz Bichero, a friendly and helpful couple who liked the island sufficiently to move there and who are now renovating a house in Santiago (tel London 020 7485 4307; or in Gomera tel 922 89 55 57; mobile 989 85 75 98; fax 922 89 55 41).

Also helpful to me in the past has been Bill Strange, a Spanish-speaking Englishman who with colleagues runs Wildnerness Walks, offering guided walks from a base in Vallehermoso (tel 922 800 732; mobile: 699 749 042; e-mail: bill@wildernesswalks.com; web: www.wilderness.com). Bill also has a space in San Sebastian and has ambitious near-future plans for an organic farm where visitors can work, for therapy sessions, herbal walks, etc.

Getting to Gomera

On arrival in Tenerife South airport, you can either take a taxi to Los Cristianos port in the Southern tip of the island (2,000 pesetas) or share one with others in the queue, or get the somewhat unreliable airport bus No. 487. The stop is a few metres to the left on coming out of the airport terminal (see the 'Bus' sign on the lamppost. The bus is supposed to leave about once an hour, but can be up to about fifteen minutes either side of this time. The bus is marked Titsa and is green with a white door. It is posted as leaving at 20 past the hour from 7.20am to 9.20pm (then referring to the 111 as the night bus at 11.15pm, 12.30 and 4.30am); an exception is that there is a bus at 2.10pm instead of 2.20pm (which bus does not go at all on Sat, Sun and festival days). The bus goes all the way through to the port at 7.20am, 9.20am, 1.20pm and 3.20pm. If it is not going to the port, be sure to insist on getting off at the first bus stop in the built-up area of Los Cristianos. One year, the driver insisted on taking us all on, a kilometre out of our way. The bus costs 225 pesetas. I have been told by the information office that if you walk a kilometre up the airport approach road (in a Westerly direction away from the sea and the terminus) you can catch the regular 111 bus from Santa Cruz to Los Cristianos (200 pesetas). We have tried this once but there was no stop as such, and the traffic goes past as such a pace, that we decided not to risk it and returned to the airport to wait for the airport bus. Nevertheless, on the return journey, we have successfully taken this 111 bus, getting out at an unmarked stop under the bridge at the junction of the main road with the airport road.

Incidentally, hitching on Gomera itself works relatively well, especially if you are not carrying a huge pack, if you are walking rather than waiting, if you have walked to the outskirts of the towns and if it is a safe place for a car to stop. Male-female couples seldom have to wait for more than a few minutes (except at afternoon siesta time or after dark); a man on his own takes longer; and two men the longest. On my own, I have several times given up trying to hitch after dark, mainly because there has been so little traffic.

Ferry, hydrofoil or flights to Gomera

Ferries and hydrofoils go from Los Cristianos port. The old Fred Olsen ferry has been replaced by a huge new 40-minute hydrofoil ferry called the Fred Olden Benchijigua Express (tel 922 62 82 31; reserves@fredolsen.es; www.fredolsen.es – their timetable can also be found on www.gomera.net/english/faehreen.htm). It leaves for Gomera from Los Cristianos at 9am, 12.30, 4pm and 8.30pm. It returns from San Sebastian at 7.30am, 10am, 3pm and 6.30pm. Prices start at 2,570 pesetas one way. You can also catch their La Palma ferry which stops off in La Gomera, taking 75 minutes to get there, leaving Los Cristianos at 7pm daily (not Saturday).

Trasmediterranea (tel 922 75 38 67; www.tranmediterranea.es) no longer operate their rival hydrofoil but they have a regular ferry (costing from 2,307 pesetas one way) leaving Los Cristianos at 8.30am and 2pm*, returning from San Sebastian at 11.45am* and 5.15pm (*these two journeys not on Saturdays).

The airport near Santiago in Gomera is now at last open, but it is more of a sweat to use it than to take the hydrofoil. It means going all the way to Tenerife North airport and then a 30 minute plane ride costing 8,000 pesetas one way. The service runs daily (except Sunday) at 8am and 4.45pm, although I suspect services will be curtailed as they must be losing money. The service is provided by Binter airlines (tel 922 635 998) whose ticket agents are Iberia (sales of tickets opposite check-in counters 26 and 27 at the South Airport in Tenerife).

There is a Fred Olsen ferry daily (but not Saturday) from San Sebastian in La Gomera to El Hierro island leaving at 8am (leaves from El Hierro on the return at 1.30pm). Trasmediterranea offer a rival ferry from Los Cristianos to El Hierro leaving daily (except Saturday) at 7.15am; on Saturdays it goes via Gomera and leaves at 8.30am.

The Hotel Andreas in the Calle General Franco, opposite the big white church in the square of Los Cristianos, not far from the main bus stops, is a possible place to stay in you get stuck overnight in Los Cristianos, costing from about 8,000 pesetas for two people for one night. Should you have to spend a longer time on Tenerife, a friend recommends the region of Macizo de Anaga in the North of the island, beyond Santa Cruz, as being beautiful and relatively unspoilt.

Stamps, telephone, internet

On one of my trips, no less than three main post offices in Gomera's towns, in Vallehermoso, Valle Gran Rey and Alajero, had no stamps suitable for postcards to the UK, and the one in Valle Gran Rey had no stamps at all ('manana'), which seemed slightly extraordinary for a post office. So if you are a multiple postcard writer like me, it might be as well to stock up on stamps as and when you find any, or in Los Cristianos. Stamps for postcards to the UK cost 75 pesetas.

You must put at least 30 pesetas in a phone box or it will cease dialling after two numbers. For all phone numbers in Gomera, even those dialled from within Gomera, you now have to add 922 in front of the old six-figure number.

San Sebastian in Gomera now has a public internet cafe (675 pesetas for 45 mins) by the waterfront: El Ambigu Cafe Internet, Plaza de las Americas 8 (tel 922 872041, ambigu_99 @yahoo.es) open Monday to Thursday 8am to 12.30 at night; Friday and Saturday from 8.30am to 2am; closed Sunday). In Valle Gran Rey there is one near the beach and tourist office: Gerardo's Internet Bar (tel 922 805122) no doubt also has this facility.

San Sebastian

On arrival in San Sebastian, head for Calle del Medio where most of the pensions are (or the road parallel to this, Calle Ruiz de Padron). For instance, the spartan and not particularly friendly but very beautiful **Pension Gomera** (Calle del Medio 33, tel 922 870417) is just before the main church, on the opposite side of the road. To get there you go to the main town square, Plaza de Las Americas, at the end of the harbour wall. If you keep to the right hand side of this plaza, you find a smaller one behind it graced with huge trees (said to be Ficus microcarpa, laurel of India) shading a café, Kiosco Las Calabellas. You take Calle del Medio, the main high street North and to the left of this square, the middle of the three roads going North. Incidentally, on the right hand side of Calle del Medio, the first house at No. 4 is the **tourist information office** (tel 922 141512; turismo @gomera-island.com), which has an incomplete list of accommodation addresses on the island, with their phone numbers and also a bus timetable.

Pension Gomera has rooms on a first floor balcony level arranged around a magical inner courtyard where you can sit out under a tall coconut palm that is surrounded by a tropical garden. The pension itself is primitive in its facilities (as are almost all the pensions in Gomera; apartments tend to be slightly better equipped). It has one toilet with a basin and an intermittent warm shower.

The pension sometimes has a full-up sign in German, when in fact it is not full, so it is still worth asking (by going upstairs to the first floor residence of the owner, or by asking in the supermarket which they run on the other side of the road next to the church). They charge 3,500 pesetas for two people for one night.

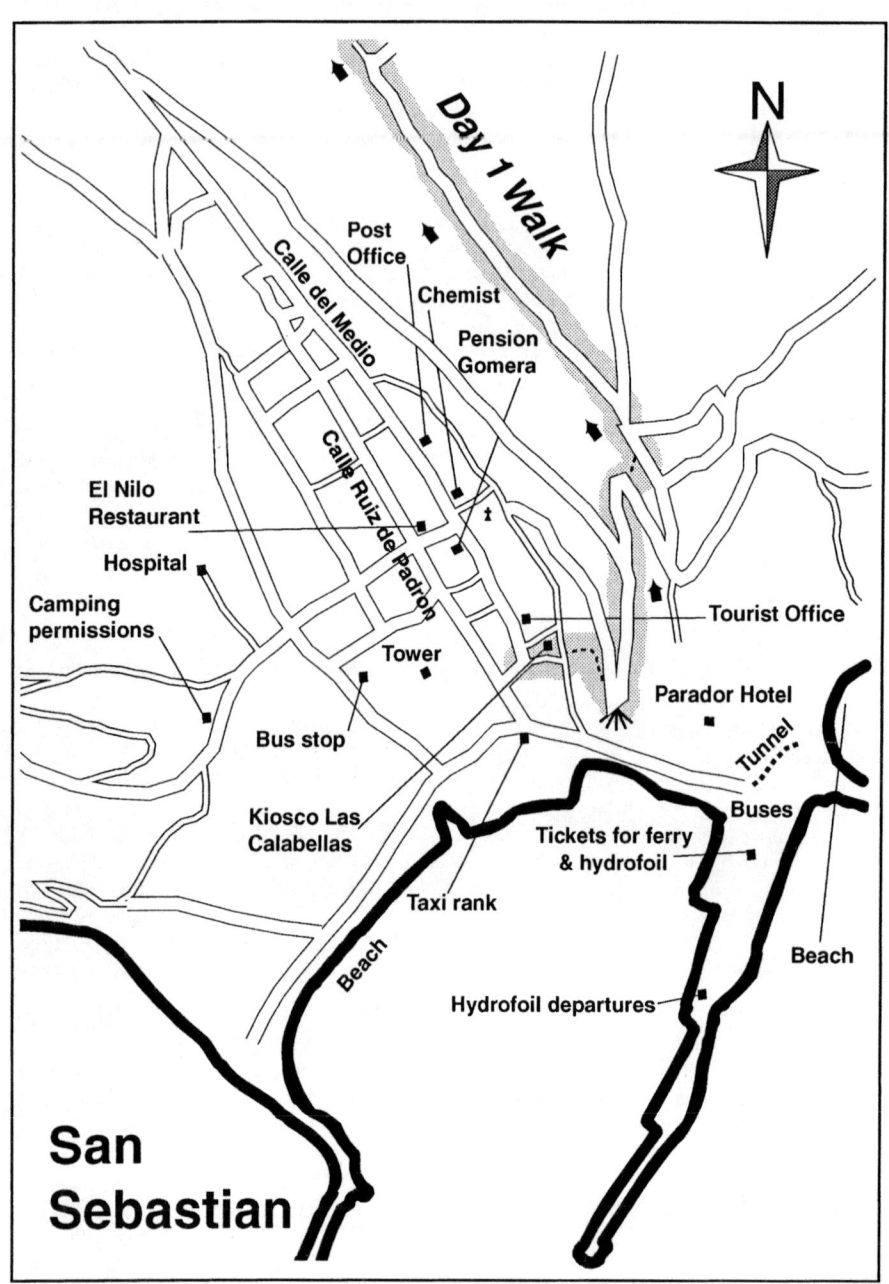

Other cheap possibilities include **Pension Victor Leralta** (in the same street, Calle Del Medio, No. 23, tel 922 871102 or 870207; 3,000 pesetas for two people for one night) or **Pension Colon** (tel 922 870235) much further up at No 59 (3,500 pesetas for two people for one night). At this pension in 2001, I spent all night fighting off mosquitoes or being kept away by the very noisy passageway. There is also the **Pension Hesperides** (Calle Ruiz de Padron 24, tel 922 871305). The Hesperides, which boasts that it is 'completely renovated' (although in fact still very primitive despite some en suite tiny bathrooms with hot water) costs 4,300 pesetas for two people for one night. They supply a towel. They may also be willing to look after your excess luggage for a week until your return journey (as may the Pension Colon). Much further up the Calle Ruiz de Padron is the Bar Restaurante **Columbina** (tel 922 871257) with a four storey pension next to it at No. 81 – it has modern rooms with no windows but en suite toilet and shower, for 3,000 pesetas for one night for one person. The tourist office also list **Villa Gomera** at Ruiz de Padron 68 (tel 922 870020) as having 20 places, at 6,000 pesetas for one night for two persons.

Apartments I have seen advertised include **Apartamentos San Sebastian** (Calle Del Medio 20, tel 922 871354) and Canarias (Calle Del Medio 3, tel 922 141453) and **Apartamentos Bazar Garcia** (Calle Del Medio 27, tel 870652). The **Parador** luxury hotel up above the town is tel 922 871100, but is way outmatched for facilities by the Hotel Tecina in Santiago. I met a couple, however, who twice had breakfast at the Parador hotel and recommended it. Since it's on the route for Day 1 (see below) it could be a way to start the day in style.

My favourite evening eating place is the slightly upmarket **Bar Restaurante El Nilo**, run by a friendly man called Mario Medina Hernandez, at Calle Ruiz de Padron 40 (tel 922 870305; turn left coming out of the Pension Gomera, first left again opposite the church, and it's there on the next corner, on your right, on the corner with Aveninda de Colon). This restaurant can be crowded. There are several other adequate ones in the same street, the best of these alternatives is probably the **4 Caminos**. There is also the much cheaper **Bar Restaurante Venezuela**, more used by local people, but a much more basic menu, at the very end of the Pension Gomera road, Calle del Medio (if heading out of town), on the right hand side, at No. 98. Or in Calle del Medio there is the Cultural Centre restaurant, the **Bar Restaurante Junonia** at No 51 (open to tourists too, offering dishes such as fish steak for 700 pesetas). Or nearer the sea on this same street, on the other side of the road, the **Restaurante Gomera Garden**, which has a nice enough ambiance with its trees and garden but serves fairly poor food.

For **Buses** from San Sebastian, go along the beachfront to the tower and turn right beyond it. The buses stop on the roadside between the tower and the petrol station, with no bus stop sign but simply wherever people gather. The bus times change to coincide with the ferries. At present all the buses leave at (* = not Sunday or festival days) 10.30am, 2pm*, 5.30pm and 9.30pm*. Line 1 goes to Degollaga de Peraza, Chipude, Las Hayas, Arure and Valle Gran Rey; Line 2 to Hermigua, Agulo & Vallehermoso; and Line 3 to Degollaga de Peraza, Las Toscas, Tecina, Playa Santiago, Alajero. But get the bus timetable from the tourist office or check locally (although on one occasion six people gave me six different times). The bus service's phone number is 922 141101. Buses leaving San Sebastian in the morning tend to be too late to be of much use for full-day walks. Buses towards San Sebastian can be more helpful.

A phone number for **taxis** in San Sebastian is 922 870524. The rank is by the beach.

Language

I get by just about adequately on the few words of pidgin

Spanish listed below, forming any other words I need by adding Spanish-sounding endings to English or French or Italian words. Pidgin Spanish must sound very blunt and rude, so be sure to throw in plenty of Por Favors and Muchias Graciases.

These key guide book phrases are, in their rough and ready order of usefulness (with my added accents showing where to stress the word):

- Por favór. (Please.)
- Múchias Grácias. (Thank you.)
- Dónde está el sendéro por camináre a [Hermígua]? (Where is the footpath for walking to [Hermigua]?)
- Hermóso (Beautiful), Sobérbio (Superb), Magnífico (Magnificent).
- Dos mántas mas, por favor. (Two more blankets please – no Gomeran pension has ever given me enough blankets without having to be asked. I do not know how most travellers survive the cold nights with just one blanket, unless they remain fully dressed.)
- Frío. (Cold.)
- Es possíbile una habitación por dos [tres, quátro]? (Is it possible to have a room for two [three, four]?)
- Por úna nóche. (For one night.)
- Cuánta cuésta? (How much does it cost?)
- La cuénta, por favór. (The bill, please.)
- Es urgénte. (It is urgent.)
- Quisierámos. (We'd like.)
- Quéso. (Cheese.)
- Sópa de berros. (A watercress soup with potatoes.)
- Almogrote. (A piquant spread of goats cheese, garlic, oil and pepper.)
- Tortílla. (Omelette.)
- Zúmo de melecotón. (Peach juice.)
- Víno de Goméra. (Gomeran wine.)
- Licér de naránja. (Orange liqueur.)
- Combinádo de frúitos sécos. (Mixed nuts and raisins.)
- Manána. (Tomorrow.)
- Hoy. (Today.)
- Ayér. (Yesterday.)
- Aríba. (Above.)
- Abájo. (Below.)
- A la Derécha (To the right.)
- A la Isquiérda (To the left.)
- Crúce. (Crossroad.)
- Todo récto. (Straight on.)
- Parada. (Bus stop.)
- Ida y vuélta. (Return ticket.)
- A que hóra sale la guágua (pronounced 'wawa') hácia San Sebastian? (What time is the bus to San Sebastian?)
- Podra ustéd depositárme el equipáje aquí duránte una semána? (Could you keep the luggage here for one week?)
- Note to send ahead with your luggage by taxi: Mandamos el equipaje par taxi, vamos a venir caminando y llegaremos sobre las 8.00. (We are sending the luggage by taxi, we are walking and will arrive at about 8.)
- Zimmer zu Vermieten. (German notice seen in windows meaning 'Rooms to Rent'.)
- 'Rte' added on to the end of the name of a bar means that it is also a restaurant.

And never yet needed, but useful in reserve:

- Socórro! (Help!)
- Herído. (Injured.)
- Un médico. (A doctor.)

Day 1 Walk: San Sebastian to Hermigua

Toughness: 8. Beauty: 6. Hours: 11.

From San Sebastian, this walk follows map route 35/36 joining map route 52 all the way to Hermigua (via El Palmar), although the last short-cut down into lower Hermigua (Santa Catalina) is only marked on more recent editions of the German map. The walking is easy but long, and as it is the first day, the 28 kilometres or so can feel more like 28 miles and tends to take our party 10 to 12 hours, going slowly, although fast walkers are said to be able to do it in 5. So it is best to set out early this first day, without dilly-dallying too much on the way, as you may not at this stage know how you are going to react to the walking, or how often you are likely to take a wrong turning, or whether your hat will stay on in the wind or if you will get heat exhaustion. Most of the first part of the walk has been upgraded with red and white slashes of paint to show the way. The second half of the walk is being upgraded to a crazy paving car road, with finishing touches being put to what seem to be tourist villas. At the time of writing, however, there is one rather run-down farmstead (Casas de Enchereda) where you *may* be able to buy cheese and get water on the way, if anyone is in. Drink plenty of liquid before you set off, if you want less to carry. Sundown is at about 6.45pm in the Winter and 9.15pm in the Summer. (In fact in Gomera we try to take advantage of daylight by getting on the way each day by 9am or shortly after, especially for this first day. And remember that the clocks go forward an hour, on the Sunday before Easter.)

If the slightest bit dubious about the length of this walk, or if wanting a pleasant and easy first day, you should shorten the walk substantially – as most of my friends seem to prefer – by just doing the first part – ie staying on routes 35 and 36 all the way – coming down to where the **Camino Forestral de Majona** meets the Carreteria del Norte TF-711 and thumbing a lift or stopping a passing taxi on this main road.

An alternative way of shortening the walk is to do only the longer second half, route 52, by getting a taxi from the seafront (or thumbing a lift) to the start of the Camino Forestral de Majona, marked on the German map, and just South of Casas de Enchereda, 7 km out of San Sebastian on the road to Hermigua. This second half of the walk is more varied than the first, which passes through high and impressive but rather bleak and arid terrain. The Camino where you begin the walk is in the next bay of roadspace on the right after the one with two little houses (a drystone wall one and one white with a little water tank above it). The bay with the Camino leading off it has a 'sharp bend to the right' signpost concreted into the ground. *The unasphalted Camino, a car road track, goes off uphill to the right*, with a 'Coto Privado de Caza' (no hunting) sign above it. *Within a hundred metres up this Camino* and with the 'sharp bend' sign still in sight, *you come to trail number 35/36 going up to the left (behind a five foot high drystone wall)*. The entrance is marked by a 'Parque Natural Majona' sign on a post. Your path heads up initially WNW/290 degrees. You can see white beehives some 200 metres straight ahead of you; and within a couple of minutes an orange and white slash of paint on a rock on your right. Keep on the main path. Within 40 to 50 minutes of setting out, you come to a ridge, pine trees, a view of Tenerife's Mount Teide (on a fine day) and *a T-junction of sorts. Take the way to the left, initially WNW/300 degrees*. The path becomes greener underfoot, and in due course rejoins the Camino car track, at which point you turn left towards Casas de Enchereda. See the asterisk below [*] for the continuation.

For those on the full walk: Assuming you have breakfast at the Kiosco La Cabalella in the main square (Plaza de la Constitucion) under the giant trees, behind to the SE you will see La Caja bank and to its right a shop, the Panaderia El Pejiar at No. 12. *Go up the steps between them, and, once up them, turn right into the paved walkway, the Camino de la Hila, to the Mirador viewpoint with its views out over the harbour. Follow the asphalted road uphill, signposted the Parador (a plush hotel). Keep on uphill at the fork in 150 metres. Then at the next 180 degree turn of the road, take the Camino de Puntallana stairs with the metal bannisters leading steeply up, staying with the upward option whenever there is a choice. At the top, turn left onto the asphalted mainish road going gently uphill, due North* (in 20 metres ignoring a fork uphill to the right). Your road, you will soon see, is called Calle de la Orilla del Llano. This is your way out of town, *follow it for nearly a kilometre to its bitter end, ignoring all turnings, and an asphalted road track will then offer a way forward towards a red and white TV mast* in the distance, your direction NW/320 degrees (this car road track begins where on the right there is a group of new terraced housing).

Wherever there is a choice of track, keep on towards

the aerial, even though this means leaving the asphalt. *Just 30 metres before the mast, fork right*, Northwards. Then, 30 metres before the house, fork left on the road track, your direction NNW/ 340 degrees; in 20 metres you pass a decorated water tank to your left hand side and head uphill between two rocks with yellow slashes. You go towards the hilltop ahead, your direction now NNW/350 degrees, passing rocks with white paint on your right hand side. (Beware that white paint on its own is often used for the boundary marks of fields, not necessarily to mark your path.)

From the top of the hill, carry on along the path, your direction due North. For most of the rest of this walk, there may still be red and white slashes on the rock guiding your way and much of this walk's description may therefore be redundant. In due course you come to two private TV aerials, 1 metre high (on your left hand side). Follow the path down over the rocks, then NW up the faint path of reddish rock, *hugging the San Sebastian valley or ridge whenever there is a choice.*

Soon you see the first small cave indentation in the rock (10 metres off to your right hand side) and a slight fork in the road – take the left one, going upwards WSW/260 degrees, in 5 metres passing a reassuring red and white slash to your left hand side. You can now see down into the San Sebastian valley. Keep going upwards on the main track.

You come to a sandy-coloured flatish rock, and the red and white slash shows the continuation of the path to the left, your direction SW/220 degrees.

Follow a couple of mini-cairns upwards to the right, *the aim being to get to the right of Jaragan summit* (marked with a black triangle on the German map).

Soon, if the weather is clear, you will see the mountain of El Teide (which we nickname Mount Fuji) on the island of Tenerife, floating serenely above the clouds, and providing a useful Easterly marker (or ENE/ 70 degrees, to be exact).

When you come opposite the farmstead, away to your right hand side, of half a dozen shacks on the far hillside, and at the moment these houses line up with the peak of El Teide, be careful to follow the reddish path uphill (marked in 8 metres by a red and white slash to your right hand side) and zigzagging, then heading roughly in the direction of the large cave ahead, although you will need in the end to go below it to the right. (Ignore one orange and white slash on the rocks at this point which would take you in the wrong direction.)

100 metres before the cave, take the right fork sharply down (marked by two mini-cairns - small piles of rocks), your direction initially SSE/ 170 degrees, in 10 metres heading back more in your previous direction (NNE/ 20 degrees). In 70 metres, beneath the cave and by a (possibly dry) small pool in the rocks, follow your onward path, your direction NE/55 degrees.

Those who have taken a slow two and a half hours to here, will probably find that the walk will in toto take the full 10 to 12 hours I envisaged in my introduction.

Now walk with El Teide mountain ahead of you and slightly to the right of you (at 1am to you, if your direction is midnight on the clockface), going slightly uphill.

Zigzag uphill, and with El Teide mountain behind you, *you come to a faint T-junction with a footpath offering right or left*. The right hand way may be blocked off with stones. *Head left and Westwards*, following red and white slashes and in the direction (NNW/350 degrees) of the huge TV aerial over on the far side of the San Sebastian valley.

You see an asphalted road down below you and veer right with the main path at the point when you can see the view back down into San Sebastian valley. Keep to the mountain path way above the road which is clearly identifiable from the horizontal vein of chalky-coloured rock (with wavy indentations from wind erosion) which follows the path's curve. *You walk towards a car park*. Way above you near the skyline (and with very audible dogs) is the **Casas (= Houses) de Jaragan** farmstead.

Heading down to the red car track below you, you scramble over rocks, and can scramble down all the way, although towards the end of the descent there is a path off to the right just before the flattish rock (and marked with a red and white slash at right angles) which makes the going easier, your direction WNW/300 degrees. You pass a sign saying Parque Natural Majona. This path offers a good shady spot on the hillside to have lunch or brunch and to take stock.

The car track is your easiest way to get down to the main road (turn left down the car track) so as to get a lift into Hermigua (or, for a harder descent, continue on to the asterisk below). If you are tired, if you have blisters coming on, or if you have taken three and a half hours to get this far and it is already 1pm, it is worth considering giving up at this stage. Slow walkers taking breaks will need up to seven and a half hours or so to walk on from this point.

Another way to save an hour or two is to ignore the next part of the route, the footpath up with its scenic and poorly-defined detour, and simply follow the main car track on your right all the way to Casas de Enchereda and beyond; rejoining the walk description below at the double asterisks.

For those on the full walk, however: Take the car track to the right for only a metre or so, and then *immediately go up off the road,* marked by a red and white slash and an arrow marked 'Herm', your direction WSW/250 degrees, *a scramble over whitish rock past a mini-cairn towards a 2m metal stake concreted into the hillside* (and which you can just see from the road track). Your general direction on from this stake is Westerly, with no clear path, keeping slightly nearer to the road track that heads downwards to the main road than to the same track heading onwards towards Casas de Enchereda. Red and white slashes should show the way. Follow along the ridge. Go up to the left of the summit immediately ahead of you, still following the red and white marks, with more of them again after the summit. Ignore a fork to the right (marked with a red and white X). 100 metres past a rock with a mini-cairn on top and a red and white slash, you come to a yellow rock flat area and go slightly left, heading SW/215 degrees, with a red and white slash 30 metres ahead, towards the huge TV aerial on the furthest horizon.

Then the route is along the side of the mountain, as if along the edge of a terrace, your direction WNW/300 degrees, above the main San Sebastian valley, with a view of the large reservoir below you (Embalse de Llano de la Villa on the German map), following an ill-defined path going NW/320 degrees to the left of the summit. By some conifers on the slopes to your right hand side, you come to a well-defined path going down to your left hand side, to a road track and asphalt road and parking place below. This is the path those on the shorter alternative walk, the trail up from the Camino Forestral de Majona, would be coming up, if they had got a lift or taxi to the Camino [*]. Your path joins it. Down is left, but, for those continuing the walk, follow this well-defined path to your NW/310 degrees, towards Enchereda.

Over the next brow you see the beginning of the date palms below you to the right that will continue up the valley all the way to Enchereda. *When your track drops down onto the Casas de Enchereda road track [**], turn left,* as directed by the red and white slash, *and continue on the track, ignoring all turn-offs, until you come to the El Palmar turn-off in 6 or 7 kilometres.*

Casas de Enchereda, so imposing on the map, is simply the one farmstead below you with its two reservoirs, its dozen black and pink pigs, its half dozen very fierce (but tethered) dogs and its abundance of goats. At this point you are about half way through the walk, with five hours more walking to go for slow walkers. One year there was nobody in at the farm, but another year the young couple opened the gate for us and we bought a smallish round cheese for 750 pesetas (at the time over 1000 in town; this was a smoked goat's cheese, indeed we could see the smoke rising through the chimneyless tiled roof of the shed where the cheese was being made) and drank some of the Gomeran wine offered us. All we really wanted was a refill for our water bottles, but this seemed the polite way of going about it.

Once on the car track again, stay on this even though it seems you are heading away from your destination for some time. Do not do what we did one year, mistaking the Enchereda mountain for the Enchereda homestead on the map. We headed up a track along the river valley to the mountain and fought our way through head high brambles, trying to retrace our steps down the mountain as darkness descended. A trail up to Enchereda mountain and round is shown on some maps that are still on sale, but this experience leads me to believe that a machete and true perseverance would be required to rediscover it. Anyway, staying on the car track, the next house you come to is on the left hand side, with a new tiled roof and two sets of double doors, and a two-door electricity box opposite the house. Later, you come to **Casas de Juel** on the map, above a small concrete reservoir and probably only partially abandoned, as the area teems with goats (I also saw some of the few cows I have seen on the island here once). A metal ramshackle gate may be closed across the road track about half a kilometre beyond Casas de Juel, but it is easy to circumvent this gate to the right. The goats get round it easily too, so I am not sure who it may be aimed at, unless it be car drivers or cows.

You pass another new house on your left hand side, virtually identical to the previous one. 200 metres beyond this, you pass a large animal enclosure made of wooden poles built around a tree, on your left, and later past a well on your right, padlocked closed, with a symbolic bucket on a pole high above it. You may need to go through a gate made of corrugated iron.

Soon you may be able to see the outskirts of Hermigua, your destination, in the far distance to your North West (but still some three and a half hours away for slow walkers). Soon you will need to look out for your car track turning right to **El Palmar**. Before you get to this turning, you will be able to see the track turning right below you, heading down into palm trees and to a partly derelict house with orange roof tiles. Before the turn, and just after crossing a small stream, you come to the first bamboo stand of the day, which might be a good place to cut your long walking stick, if you have by now decided that such might be helpful. Next, *5 metres before a blue stopcock on the main pipe and with a red 'X' painted ahead of you, and with above you a house on the hillside, turn sharp right off your road, heading to El Palmar*, due East, towards El Teide mountain.

You pass the same abandoned house you saw from above, which has giant geranium bushes in the front garden (and past a white and rusted Morris 1000 wreck on your right). Then you go past a concrete house on your left which has a sign on its far side saying Palmar de Agen. Next after this, you see below you the farmhouse you will be heading for, in a group of palm trees, and with a couple of outhouses. The turn-off to it is an ill-defined path on your left, where you can scramble down towards the farmhouse (you could follow the car track and then turn left along another car track – this is simply a short-cut). The turn-off comes just after the dark black terraces with their vineyards (which seem to offer a way down of their own), down reddish rock, and is an easy scramble down (just before you get down to the road track leading to this house, head left towards the streambed to make the scramble easier).

Take the road track past the farmhouse, which again says Palmar de Agen on its far side. *When the road track comes to an end, continue onwards on a faint track heading NNW/340 degrees through palm trees and pasture-like fields*, studded with dark boulders, a pleasant spot for a picnic. Slow walkers will be some three hours out of Enchereda at this stage.

You come to two palm trees and you can see the continuation of your path on the hillside ahead curving along the hillside. Make your way down over a streambed, over a new a bridge with green metal railings, follow some terraces and mini-cairns to the right round the hillside. Below you is the **Playa de la Calita**, a small black sand bay, said to be a good place for a dip, with a little chapel, the **Ermita de San Juan**, some boats and a palm tree.

Your onwards track follows parallel to the approach car track to this beach (don't be tempted by a path downwards to the right towards a white footbridge below). Carry on WNW/290 degrees along the left side of the valley. Your aim is to join the beach road approach track up ahead; which means crossing a streambed down on your right and then up the other side. *So you head down towards the croaking frogs, and at the T-junction you turn right,* as directed by the red and white slashes, *going over the stream on a bridge with green metal railings,* and following the path up to the tarmac road.

Then turn left on this car road and follow its bends for one and a quarter kilometres.

You come to a sharp bend to the right, over an arched drystone and concrete bridge, carrying a wide pipe under the road, with way above it on the horizon a green and yellow sign. Here, if you would like a short-cut, *go over the bridge and at its far edge, take the path that goes steeply upwards towards the sign,* your direction WNW/285 degrees – a path with widely-spaced steps

The green and yellow sign, when you get to it, says Playa La Caleta one way and Montoro, El Palmar and Tagaluche the other. Turn right on the road for 20 metres, and go left down the well-defined path.

You have a view out, if you look over the edge, onto Santa Catalina or lower Hermigua – this is where route 52 goes sharp left, at the rejoining with the El Moralito branch of 52. This is your substantial short-cut down. The path leads downhill and is an initially NE direction. Keep on the main path.

The path leads past telegraph poles to concrete steps heading to your right down to the bridge. *Cross the bridge,* with the banana plantation on your right.

Hermigua

Now you are in lower Hermigua (Santa Catalina). Going on past the **Bar Restaurant Los Pismas** on your left (there are steps up to this), at the first junction you turn left (the right turn is your car track for tomorrow towards Lepe. If you have excess energy, you could go on at this stage via Lepe to Agulo, see below, to be at the start the next day's walk). You go up past the **Bar El Piloto** on your left at number 16. This is the best place to stop for a drink for the next kilometre or so. Rooms cost 2,000 pesetas for one night for two people. In 1995 and 2000, we stayed in Ramon's **Apartamento Santa Catalina** (which has some hot water), in (lower) Hermigua, opposite and above the Bar Piloto, up some concrete-bannistered steps. 6,000 pesetas for four people for one night (Ramon or his wife Chelo, tel 922 880700; fax 992 880700. Ramon's mobile is 670 65 41 44). Ramon also runs the local **taxi** service. (Bar Piloto maybe doesn't get on with Ramon and told us that Ramon's apartments were full when they weren't.) Another local taxi is run by Manuel Cordera Leon, tel 922 880916, mobile 636 243146, a very kind old man who has helped us beyond the call of duty.

Going on up the main road past Bar Piloto, you pass the **El Faro Bar Restaurant** (often closed). Then up past a derelict mansion on the right, No. 3, unmarked but known as **Pension Castellana** (3 Carretera de la Playa, tel 922 880008 or 880230) was closed when I passed it in 2000 and 2001, possibly temporarily, but was adequate in 1998, at 2,000 pesetas for two for one night. A floorboard had given way, the plumbing was dodgy, the water was cold (my theory is that many of these pensions are run by widows who have no husband to do the handyman jobs for them) but the ceilings were high and there was a lovely inner courtyard on the first floor of plants and fruit trees and even a splendid cactus chandelier.

If you are planning to follow the walks in this guide, you will be returning to

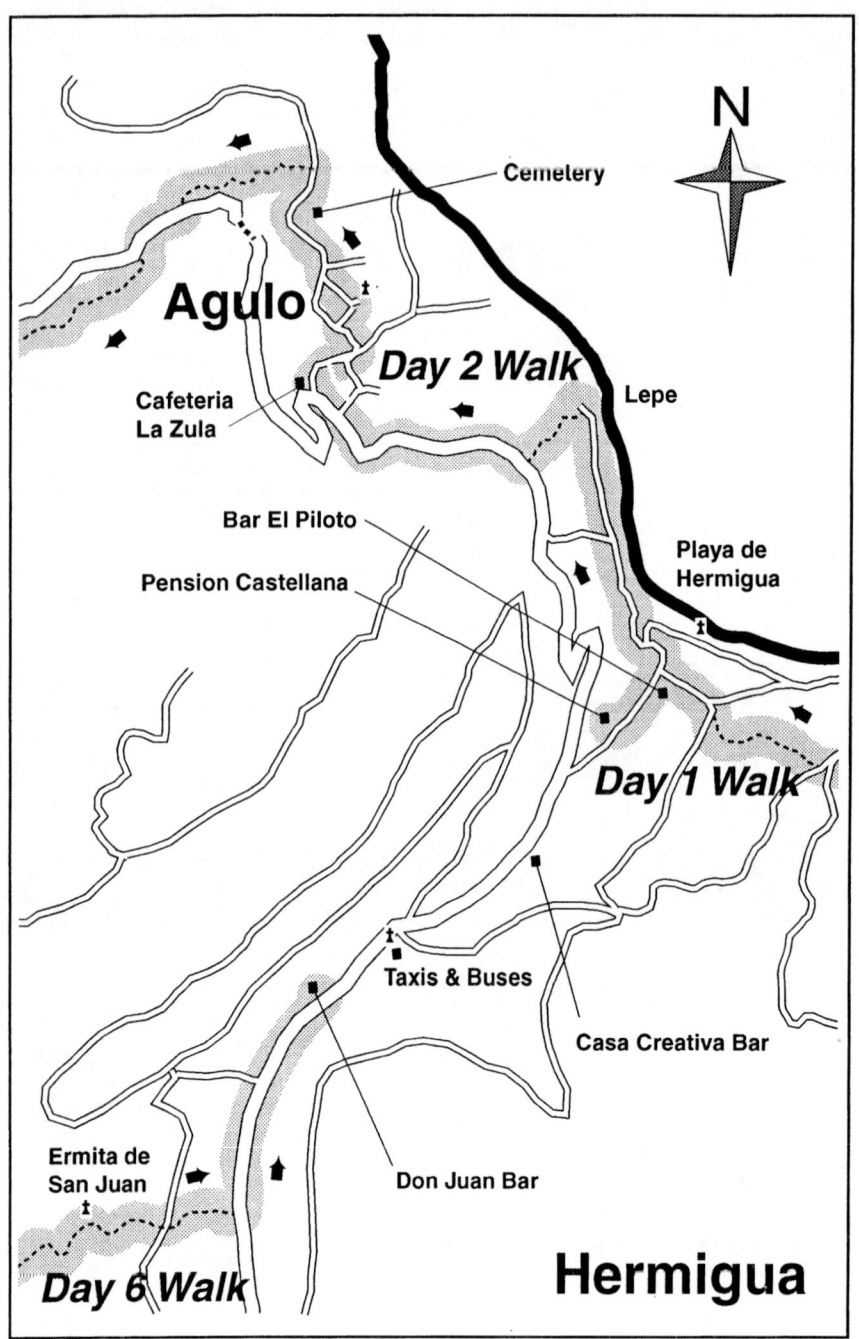

Hermigua on Day 6, so if you have now found by experience that your pack is far too heavy, you may be able to negotiate to leave some items at your pension for a few days.

Other possible cheap places to stay include **Pension-Bar Cuca**, Calle San Pedro 7; **Appartamentos Los Telares** at El Convento, 6 Ctra. General, tel 922 880781, 4,000 pesetas for two people for one night; and, more expensive, 'but beautiful and run by a nice German woman' is **Helga Grossman**'s place, where you can do your own cooking, at Carratera General 72 (tel 922 881040). The tourist office also lists as apartments: **Playa** (Playa Sta. Catalina 21, tel 922 144064; fax 922 880276) for 3,500 pesetas for two people for one night; **Casa Margot** (Ctra. Los Gomeros 12, tel 922 87 09 79); **Hotel Villa de Hermigua** (tel 922 880317).

The trendy place to eat is **Casa Creativa** (Carretera General 56, tel 922 881023) another five minutes uphill from Pension Castellana (beyond where the beach road has merged with the road coming from Agulo). It is on the left of the road, just past the arts and crafts centre on the right. Casa Creativa is a friendly German semi-health-foods type place, with herbal teas and tiny portions of salads in the bar and a restaurant downstairs. A few guide books are available at the nearby arts shop, **Capitol**, Carretera General 195 (tel 922 880253). Casa Creativa is open daily (close Saturday) from about 9am to 11pm. Its guests have mainly prebooked from Germany, paying about 6,000 pesetas per day for two.

Buses go to Agulo and Vallehermoso from near the main church and taxi rank at (*= not Sunday or festival days) 11.15am, 2.45pm*, 6.15pm, 10.15pm* (5 minutes later from down by La Castellana). Buses also go the other way, to San Sebastian, at 6.30am*, 9am, 2pm* and 5pm (10 minutes earlier down by La Castellana). A **taxi** to San Sebastian costs 3,000 pesetas.

Agulo

Agulo is a more beautiful place than Hermigua and is also the start of Day 2's walk, so if you still have the energy at the end of Day 1, you may prefer to try for accommodation there. If accommodation in lower Hermigua is not available, my preference is to take a bus or taxi on to Agulo. We used to stay in an old couple's house directly in front of the church entrance, who have since died. It is apparently still possible to do so (for 2000 pesetas for two people for one night) via the caretaker, **Senora Mercedes**, although she is not often there. Ask for her house, which is up this street in front of the church, Calle de Pedro Bettencourt, then second left, 10 metres on the right. Also possible, although more expensive, is **Apartamentos Bajip** (tel 922 146129) at Piedra Grande 4 in Calle Pintor Aguilar (beyond the pharmacy, mentioned in Day 2 below, you turn right by a sign to the Apartamentos Bajip, with another sign by the actual apartment, which is near the end of the warren of passageways. They cost 4,000 pesetas for two people for one night); or try **Petra and Pedro** (c/o La Puntilla s/u, tel 922 146028, or ask in one of the bars for Petra, such as in the Restaurant La Zula, which is near the start of the road from Hermigua to Agulo – see map). There is also an elegant award-winning 'hotel rural'. **Casa de los Perez** in the centre of Agulo at Piedra Grande 20, tel 922 146122 (although we could get no answer on the phone in 2001). This costs 5,000 pesetas for one night for two people.

Buses go (*= not Sunday or festival days) to Vallehermoso via Las Rosas from Agulo at 11.45am, 3.15pm*, 6.45pm and 10.45pm*. Buses also go the other way, to San Sebastian via Hermigua at 6am*, 8.30am, 1.30pm* and 4.30pm.

Agulo **taxi**: 922 880931 (or call one from Hermigua, qv).

Day 2 Walk: Hermigua to Vallehermoso

Toughness: 6. Beauty: 8. Hours: 9.5.

This walk is about 15 kilometres and is, in summary, a

long initial climb (largely in the shade if you go up in the morning) rewarded by a longer, more beautiful descent. For those walking slowly with lots of breaks, it could take as much as nine and a half hours (allowing for two hours at the Visitors Centre). Once you get to Agulo the route is along the Northern branch of the German map's route No. 31, reaching the Visitors Centre (and bar opposite) in time for lunch, then on along route 50, and later onto the Southern branch of route 24/25 from El Tion down through a beautiful valley of date palms into Vallehermoso (Spanish for the aptly named 'Valley Beautiful').

There is a steep climb of up to an hour and a half from Agulo out of the barranco. The faint-hearted might like to shorten the walk by taking a taxi or thumbing a lift to the Visitors Centre (called in Spanish 'Juego de Bolas' = 'Game of Bowls'; and also 'Centro de Visitantes'); then almost the whole of the rest of the day will be downhill. (Or take a bus to Las Rosas and walk up the road for 3km to the Visitors Centre.)

If you eat lunch, there is a just adequate bar with food by the visitor's centre (but is closed on Mondays). Friendlier is the Bar-Restaurante Juego de Bolas, about 250 metres further on – see directions below (or you could detour to the attractive bar restaurant at Las Rosas).

A pleasant place to buy food for the day and refill water bottles is Agulo.

For those on the full walk: There is a seafront path to Agulo from Hermigua via Lepe not marked on the German map but straightforward enough. It's back down towards the beach, *past El Piloto bar, turn left by the shrine and go all the way to the beach front. Turn left along this sea front and soon up the tarmac road towards the village of Lepe*, still following the sea front. *In Lepe village turn left by the first house you come to on your left hand side, up the concrete steps and heading up to the highway above* (in a SW direction). It is straight up, following the line of the street lamps.

At the top, turn right onto the main road into Agulo. Once in the town (where to go right would bring you to the Panaderia supermarket) *fork left*, coming in 150 metres to a telephone box on your left hand side (about 40 metres below the **Cafeteria La Zula** which is on the bend of the road above you; we sometimes have breakfast there). By the box, *turn right on the paved road opposite the Cafe*, your direction NNE/30 degrees. This is Calle Alameda. You pass Alameda shop and café on your left hand side, and a credit card bank machine on your right hand side and a pharmacy, and then a sign to Apartamentos Bajip. *Turn left at the fork, uphill, and you come directly to the church square.* (The church square bench makes another good spot to eat breakfast.) *Going past the front of the church,* *with the tourist office on your left hand side, you continue upwards along the Calle de Pedro Bettencourt*, your direction NW/325 degrees.

You can see out to the right, above the beach on the far hillside, the town cemetery that you need to head for – the walled cemetery with its four storeys of internment chambers (worth a visit). So *at the top of the street, turn right, Northwards, towards the cemetery* along a cobbled road.

About 30 metres beyond the cemetery, turn left up a broad track, your direction NNE/15 degrees, a steady, relatively easy upwards track.

Soon you can see an asphalt road below you. Within about 12 minutes of starting up the track, *you come to an asphalt road, with a tunnel, the Tunel de Agulo, on your left. You turn right*, Westwards, *and after 150 yards take the path upwards* (your direction SW/235 degrees; it has a green arrow pointing up). You are going up towards the telegraph poles on the hillside, with the path marked by greed dots (and later by a few faded red dots). Keep on the main track, still more or less following the route of the asphalt road below you.

Within about 30 minutes from the tunnel, *you come to a big house with pillars, built above a tall terrace, with a concrete front fence. The path goes round the back of this house, but before you come to the end of the house at the back, turn left, signposted Palmita, by a cairn up a path,* initially ESE/105 degrees. A green dot on the trail after 15 metres reassures you that you are on the right path.

Within 15 minutes of this house, you are at the top, and cairns and green dots lead you into a wind-blown concrete-coloured lava trench – eucalyptus trees, which cut out the sunlight and whose fallen leaves are acidic, thus preventing undergrowth that would stabilise the soil, have caused this erosion. You follow a well-defined path along the left hand side of the trench with mud steps. *Beyond the trench, continue slightly to your left on a red earth car-wide trail;* your direction SW/225 degrees. Within a couple of minutes another red earth trail joins yours from behind you on the left. There is an asphalt road below you. You continue on down to this asphalt road, and the vast and plush **Visitors' Centre** is immediately on your right, with its entrance opposite the **bar**. (For the **Bar-Restaurante Juego de Bolas**, which I prefer, follow the walk directions below, but in 200 metres take the first fork left not right. It is open daily except Tuesday from 9am to 9pm.)

It can take three hours from Hermigua to here, if going slowly and stopping for breakfast in Agulo.

The Centre, open daily 9.30am to 4.30pm (tel 922 800993) and closed December 25th and January 1st, has displays about the history of the island, books in Spanish (some other books in English are for sale in one of the workshops), a mock-up of a Gomeran house and a relatively interesting and regularly shown film about the island, normally shown whenever a coach party turns up, complete with subtitles to the whistling language (you can try asking them to show the film in English). The Centre's garden has displays with name plates of the island's main, trees plants and bushes. For me it adds to the interest of the walks to learn the names of some of the commonest vegetation, and to make drawings of these in my notebook. The ones I have drawn and thereafter began to recognise include Tabaiba dulce (Euphorbia balsamifera), Bejeque (Aeonium subplanum) and Cardon (Euphorbia canariensis – which is poisonous to touch, incidentally).

From the Centre our walk is route 50. *Coming out of the Centre's gate, turn right, heading out on the tarmac road to the SSW/200 degrees,* and, in 200 metres, *taking the first fork right signposted Laguna Grande.* In about 400 metres up this fork, there is a track to the right marked 'Privado'. Do not take this (it leads down to the Las Rojas restaurant). Your trail is to the right some way on, within about 8 minutes from the Centre, *just before the road makes a sharp bend to the right* (opposite the driveway to a white house on your left hand side, where telephone cables cross the road) *turn right through a red and white barrier at the top of the path,* your direction West/275 degrees. *80 metres in, you cross a tarmac road.* Having crossed the car road track, you *go immediately quarter right,* your direction SW/235 degrees, down a faint trail, a green chain fence to your left hand side, and, down, in 20 metres passing a telegraph pole, and going on down. The trees are mainly laurel and tall heather (Erica arborea). You go over a stream, and up steps the other side towards a house painted pink with green windows (called Sabina). Passing the left hand side of this house, you go straight up, soon alongside a fenced vineyard on your left hand side. *Follow the field to your left hand side and follow the path as it curves left.* Head West along the ridge with two electricity pylons visible to your right. Keep to the main path (a left fork goes to a house) with soon a terrace wall to your left hand side, your direction Westerly/275 degrees.

Do not go quite up to the pylons; your path continues straight over the junction you meet by the pylons, running slightly leftwards WSW/240 degrees, following parallel to the pylon cables (to their left hand side).

You see below you to the right hand side, the road along the top of the reservoir dam which you must cross in due course. *At the solitary pylon, a path goes down to the right.* Take it, your direction NW/310 degrees. (It has steps cut coming down from above you.)

Head downwards – you are aiming for the house furthest to the right.

Keep to the main path (which becomes a car road track) until you come to this last house, on your left hand side (where the road you are on veers sharply right) then go *left down the side of this house*, on concrete steps to the reservoir dam of the **Embalse de Amalhuigue**.

Go across the dam, and turn left along the asphalt road for three kilometres or so. Eventually you come to the **Bar Bodegon** on your right hand side, a bar with a stunning view (tel 922 800483, open 9am to 9pm, and welcoming enough to those stopping for a drink, as long as they are not busy serving meals). Just past the bar, you come to a paved look-out area or mirador on your right hand side, with two street lamps. It is as if you were on a ridge between two valleys, and you can now see the Vallehermoso valley, with the town in the distance. You can also see your continuation path on the hillside opposite and the far house (to the SW/245 degrees) from which you will make your eventual descent.

In 25 metres, *you come to a threefold fork in the road, take the car road track to the right*, your direction SSW/210 degrees, down towards **El Tion** on the map. The road turns into a trail some dozen minutes from the fork. Keep on the main trail. Within five minutes of the footpath-size path, you come to a house with a red circle on its wall and a red arrow out from the circle indicating go left. Don't. *Go down the right hand side of the house, a wooden railing to your right hand side, and you can see a path heading NNW/345 degrees* along a narrow promontory of land in the general direction of Vallehermoso, with an aqueduct leading into this path.

I always like to stop for a picnic just below this house. You can see the whole valley below you (and the car road track you will be joining later, way below you to your NW).

Your route onwards is down the promontory trail and you then *stay on the main trail down, reaching the car road track within twenty minutes and turning left onto this*. Just before entering town on this road, you pass the office and home of Bill Strange of Wilderness Walks (it may have a sign up or ask local people), who in 2000 helped us find special price accommodation in Vallehermoso at the Hotel de Triana (see his details under Guided Walks in the introduction).

Walking down this beautiful valley, within thirty minutes you can see most of the town, and even the town square in the far distance, and *your road crosses a path with green railings going up and going down. Take the one to the left, going down the concrete steps*.

At the bottom you go left onto the asphalt road, and then along the right hand side of the playground with the hideous modern statues, and left up to the main road and square.

Vallehermoso

The best bar in the square to ask for accommodation is called **Bar Rte Amaya**. They phone up for you to the pension next door at No 2 (Pension Amaya, 2 Plaza de la Constitucion, tel 922 800073 or 800077). Here if you ask for a room at the back (2400 pesetas for two people for one night) you have the sound of running water and very noisy frogs – it is either that or the front rooms and the noise of traffic. As usual in Gomera, the pension is friendly and the plumbing primitive.

A friend of mine stayed happily at the **Pension Casa Bernardo**, Calle Triana 4 (the road going up right as you come out of Bar Rte Amaya, tel 922 800849). Bernardo is readily recognisable as a very gentle, distinctively short man, of tiny build, with a high pitched voice, a pointed beard and green eyes. A room costs 4,000 pesetas for two people for one night.

Another cheap possibility is the **Hostal Vallehermoso** (tel 922 800283), Calle Triana 11, opposite the post office. A room costs 3000 pesetas for two people for one night; the beds tend to be uncomfortable, although the place is being done up so this may change; there is a shared kitchen – with the more luxurious bedroom leading off this.

Bill Strange (see half a

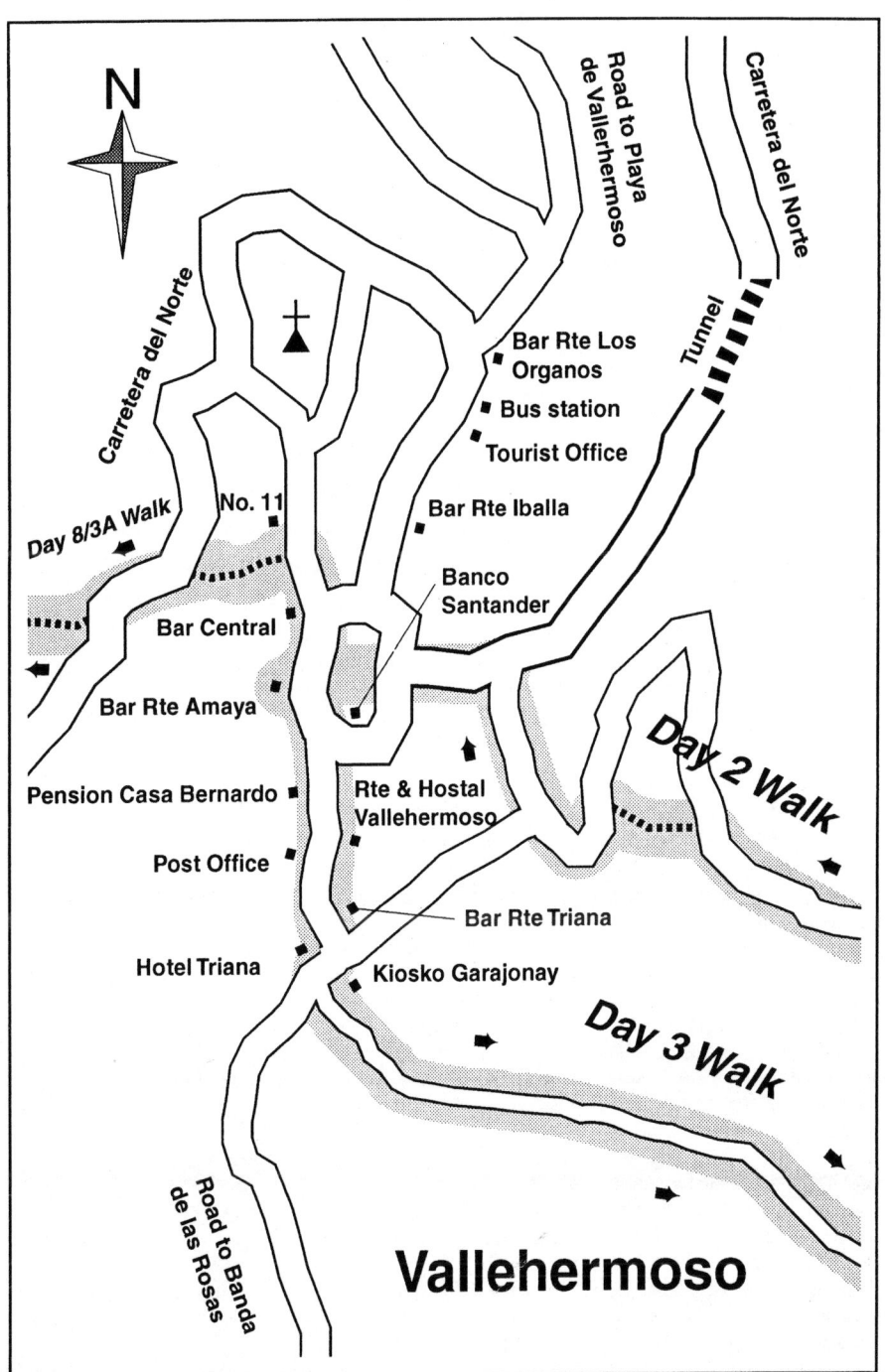

dozen paragraphs above) helped us get a cheap room for two for one night (normally 6,500 pesetas) at the new, beautifully designed and fairly luxurious Hotel de Triana in Vallehermoso (tel 922 80 05 28, e-mail: hoteltriana@teleline.es). It is opposite the Bar Rte Triana on my map. (Bill may also be able to help with other accommodation locally.)

Pension Central, Medina Hdez., Plaza de la Constitucion (tel 922 800023) has rooms for 3,000 pesetas for two people for one night.

Apartamentos Paco el Taxista – for this you ask at the **Kiosco Garojonay**, which is at the very end of the Calle Triana road – the road that has the Pension Casa Bernardo in it (see above) – heading in an out-of-town direction.

The best place to eat out, and probably for the time being the best restaurant on the island, is at **Hostal Vallehermoso**, Calle Triana 9 (open 4pm to 10.30pm). Reserve a place as it is small and is often full by 8.30pm. Garlic chicken and other delicacies are prepared by a chef who claims that he enjoys his work so much he returned to it from retirement.

Otherwise the next best bet, despite its slightly depressing feel, is the large restaurant at the back of **Bar Rte Amaya** or have snacks at the Kiosco Garojonay, or go to **Bar Restaurante Triana**, a small place to its left, or suffer the harsh lighting at the **Bar Restaurant Iballa** at 10 Avenida Guillermo Ascanio M. Greno, which is a bit hidden away off the main square – it's a road to the right of the Caja Canarias bank, and the restaurant is 80 metres along on your right. Beyond the restaurant on the right hand side is the tourist office.

There are two other restaurants in town, the **Bar Cafeteria Chamiri** (Venezuelan), at No 10 on the road towards the church and **Los Organos** (on the way to the beach, on your right hand side, at a junction below the village. Open on Sundays. ('Good, simple food' says Nick Hilborne.).

The latter is near a new **bus** terminal which it is said will in due course provide a bus service to Valle Gran Rey. At present the bus from Vallehermoso leaves at (*= not Sunday or festival days) 5.30am*, 8am, 1pm* and 4pm to Agulo, Hermigua, and San Sebastian (line 2). The bus journey to San Sebastian takes one hour and 45 minutes. The line 4 bus to Chorros Epina and Alojera goes at 2pm*.

Day 3 Walk: Vallehermoso to Chipude

Toughness: 8. Beauty: 9. Hours: 9.5.

Day 3 offers much beauty and some risk. This walk is about 18 kilometres, starts on picturesque route 23 out of town, goes down the East side of the reservoir (Embalse de la Encantadora); it then joins the asphalt road to Banda de las Rosas, goes up on a track from outside this village, the German map's route 21, coming to the reservoir Presa de Los Gallos (South West of Banda de las Rosas). From there you follow an often wet and initially brambly track, route 18 (some form of leg protection is desirable) South South West/200 degrees from the reservoir through the misty laurel forest (this is one of the most likely times on Gomera to need a mac, and the walk also involves a stretch towards the end with a 20 metre easy enough rock climb, but is a wild walk through the Parque Nacional de Garajonay and with beautiful views in clear weather). You rejoin the main road (Carretera del Centro on the German map) just to the East of Quemado summit, some 50 metres from the crossroad marked Cruz de la Hayas. Then it is a very pleasant and easy walk down routes 48 and 10 to a remarkably slow and inevitably huge lunch at the eccentric Bar Montana in Las Hayas (minimum one and a half hours), followed by paths (route 7 then 9) with gentle enough inclines to the high village of Cercado, where potters still do not use the wheel, and on (by route 4 to the West of the highway) to the village of Chipude, up almost in the clouds, which has a very primitive and Wild West flavour to it, and is the evening's destination for eating and sleeping. Allowing for lunch, getting lost once or twice, and delays at the potteries, it could take up to nine and a half hours.

Those who want a shorter and easier alternative, could miss out the route 23 scenic detour at the start, either just by walking along the road towards Banda de las Rosas or by getting a taxi (800 pesetas) or hitching from Vallehermoso for the 8 kilometres up the asphalt road to Banda de las Rosas and start from there.

The route from Presa de los Gallos steeply up through the forest is given in some of the German guides and you will occasionally meet walkers, but the Parque Nacional is apparently discouraging people from using other than its couple of main trails. This particular trail, however, seems to me a national tourist asset, one of the most stunning on the island. Presumably the main purpose of the ban is to put hunters off, but you should be aware that you are not acting in accordance with the Parque's wishes in following this route, and you may not have other travellers to call on if you run into problems – it would *not* be a good trail to do on your own. You should obey the park's code of conduct which specifies no fires (a large area of forest was burnt down in one serious incident in recent years), no camping (you need a permit – see the front of this guide), pets on a lead, respect for plants and rocks, no rubbish and no radios or music.

For an alternative and entirely permitted walk that skirts the park and is longer (22km), whilst being easier and almost equally beautiful (although it has moments where the path runs alongside steep drops, and would not be suitable on a very windy day or for anyone who has a marked fear of heights), see the Day 3 Alternative B below. This takes path 21 out of Vallehermoso to the tourist coach restaurant at Chorros de Epina, and then route 13, a road, with later a footpath to Arure (the last part of route 13, marked in green on the German map, is particularly fine). From Arure, path 10 catches the fringes of the forest and rejoins the main Day 3 walk at the Bar Montana in Las Hayas.

From Las Hayas, if you insist on visiting Valle Gran Rey, which the main walks in this book avoid, you can turn to the Day 3 Alternative A (below) for the continuation from Bar Montana. This involves going steeply downhill via the Southern branch of route 7 to Los Descansaderos; then the German map's route 3 towards Ermita de los Royes, and across the streambed and up La Calera into the heart of Valle Gran Rey.

Here are the full details **for those on the main walk:** Leave **Vallehermoso**. As if coming out of the Bar Rte Amaya, turn right and *head up out of town Southwards on the road to the right of the Banco Santander* towards the post office and Centro de Higiene Rural. Follow the road round to the right at the Kiosko Garajonay and *take a first left downhill past the road signs saying '6T' and '2'40'''*. This route is known as **Lomo Pelado** (see the German map), so you can ask local people for it by this name if you get lost. Follow the road track as it bends down to the left (past a reservoir wall on your right), and uphill the other side. Head uphill and to the right, the way being parallel to the valley bottom below. The aim eventually is to rejoin the asphalt road on the other side of the valley to your right – a road which you are presently roughly parallel to.

When the car road comes to an end by a breeze block reservoir to your right hand side, *carry on up the path*, soon with a metal railing to your left hand side, your direction ESE/120 degrees. You are then following the top edge of the valley, again parallel to the main road on the other side of the valley. When the railings come to an end, carry on along the footpath, your direction SSE/160 degrees. At a fork in 100 metres, ignore the lower right hand fork going almost straight on, and *take the left hand fork upwards*, your direction, your direction SE/140 degrees. You are about 5 metres above an aerial waterpipe that runs parallel to your path.

You continue zigzagging up and up, until you are above a little white house with a red flat roof below you to Southwards on your right hand side.

Continue on up. Keep to the left here of the summit ridge or outcrop of rock above you. Within about 30 minutes from the town square, you are now seeing down on your left into the valley of the 1000 palms which, if you were following this guide's main itinerary, you walked down into from El Tion yesterday – there is a reservoir immediately below you in that valley, at NNE/30 degrees. *Scramble up a rock to the right of the summit, to go due South.* (Do not go ESE/110 degrees, on a faint trail downwards to the left of the summit, ie not down into yesterday's valley.) A white arrow pointing towards you after 30 metres (on your left) may reassure you that you have found the right trail. You are between the two valleys. Keep on up if you face a choice. On the next ridge, with the town square below you to your NW/325 degrees, you *fork slightly left*, your direction Southwards/170 degrees, *back into yesterday's valley for 3 minutes.*

Soon you are more or less following the ridge and two thin waterpipes. Ignore paths off to the left at the next summit and *keep following the waterpipes* Southwards/190 degrees *into today's valley.*

Less than an hour after setting out, *you are now on the ridge at the top looking down at the huge reservoir, Embalse de la Encantadora. Ignore the attractions of the defined path to your left and the promising promontory to your right, and head straight over and down,* your direction SSE/160 degrees, *on a very steep path towards the reservoir.* (I have erected a mini-cairn to mark this.) Your initial direction is due South towards a phallic rock on the horizon. The path down is easy enough although overgrown. On the way down, keep to the right at the first sign of a fork – your path is overgrown – and *head towards the palm trees below; and when at the level of the top of the tallest palm tree, your overgrown path turns left briefly. Once at the palm trees, head in the general direction of the reservoir wall.* The path is ill-defined. When it becomes impossibly overgrown in your streambed, head at 2am to your present midnight direction, over a rock, Westerly, and find your onward path. Soon it goes along 5 metres above the top right hand edge of a vineyard and come out just below the reservoir wall. *Scramble up the rockside on your left to reach the wall, and then up steps and along a path on the left (Eastern) side of the reservoir, heading South on a road trail that soon becomes asphalted.* The shade of the embankment and palm trees is a good spot for a break.

Keeping to the side of the reservoir, you pass on the far side an attractive tiny island with a charming statue of a man fishing (or at least clasping a rod of some kind).

At the end of the reservoir, in front of a white forbidding reservoir building, you cross over the reservoir and head up the concrete steps opposite, Westwards, up to the main road, and turn left onto this.

You pass fields below you that seem more productive and varied in their produce than anywhere else on the island. And within 20 minutes of joining this asphalt road, keeping on upwards, you come to the hamlet of **Banda de las Rosas**. Within 30 minutes of being on this new road, you come to a small shrine (labelled San Juna) on the right hand side of the road. Keep on the main road as it continues to the left. Soon *on your right is a large waterpipe going in your direction. You follow it (rather than the main road which crosses a little concrete bridge ahead and bends left), going straight on up some concrete steps heading into the valley towards the reservoir Presa de Los Gallos* (initially in a direction that is WSW/255 degrees). *150 metres in, just before the second palm tree, it is necessary to fork uphill,* your direction WNW/285 degrees, *abandoning the water pipe.* (The way straight on is very brambly and finally impassable as I have learnt to my cost in the past.)

You do several zigzags following this path, but end up parallel to the streambed of the valley. *Within about seven minutes from this fork, you come to another, and take the left hand one,* heading WSW/255 degrees (where the right fork goes upwards, Westwards/280 degrees). Keep on the main trail that seems to lead to the obvious continuation on the hillside ahead.

You come to a minute waterfall on your right (the inside of half a bamboo stick acts as its conduit), and then you go upwards again on your trail. (For future orientation: you can see on the hillside in the distance straight ahead, the horizontal and pronounced path, leading leftwards towards the reservoir that you are making for.)

You will see high terrace walls ahead. When you are still 50 metres away, look to your left in a Southwards direction and you can see a small red-tiled house above you, and behind it the reservoir wall which is your interim destination.

The route is hard to see and overgrown, so be extra careful at this point. *Follow the trail down below the final terrace*, do not take the more obvious path up the terrace to your right; you want a very faint path, initially ESE/100 degrees towards two large metal-banded palm trees in the direction of the reservoir, *a path that then goes round outside to the right below the terrace. The trail follows below the terrace wall and looks overgrown.* But press on, it is not particularly brambly and looks worse than it is. It ends with the bamboo stand. You go over a mini-stream (within two minutes of the terrace fork) and up, with a large waterpipe accompanying you down below for a few metres. Your path is now heading SSE/160 degrees, with the reservoir wall now clearly visible. For the easiest and least overgrown of several possible final approach paths to the reservoir, *turn left once past a terrace field 200 metres below the reservoir, along the far side wall of the terrace, and go down a couple of feet to join a clear path which leads up the centre of the valley, your direction Southwards/190 degrees.*

Go right up to the reservoir wall, over a pipe, till you are five metres from the small tunnel entrance at its base. *Now go to your sharp left* in an initially ENE direction (70 degrees) – you can see the very overgrown continuation uphill. Press through as best you can, keeping carefully on the path (there is a sharp drop to your left) and continue to zigzag upwards. Follow directions carefully on this climb through the laurel forest – it is all relatively straightforward but there are two or three places where you could go off course.

(A waterpipe serves as your main reassurance, and you will be either crossing or recrossing it or walking alongside it.)

Your zigzag upwards leads you back alongside above the left side of the reservoir, the black pipe on your left for a few metres. Soon *you come to a possible fork in the path, and keep left,* your direction ESE/120 degrees initially (where the right fork is WSW/250 degrees initially) There is a small wall of mossy grey rock on your right. You come to a fine view of a high but very thin waterfall on your right – you are now at half the height of the waterfall.

Keep to the overgrown main trail, upwards, crossing the black pipe, and doing so again as you 'zig' back, and then alongside it for some minutes – you are now along the side of the valley heading SW/220 degrees towards high wooded mountain peaks ahead.

You cross a streambed (within 9 minutes of the waterfall), and the pipe goes off left, but your path goes right, initially in a NNW/340 degrees direction – in 2000 we had to crawl through fallen tree branches – and you zigzag back to head SSE/160 degrees, crossing over the pipe, and *again over a tiny streambed. Soon you are alongside the stream, heading up*, SSE/160 degrees, initially with the stream on your right hand side, later to your left.

The continuation of the route is quite evident (initially ESE/110 degrees) and upwards. 5 minutes later you have a fine view back over the valley you have come from, and a platform of flat rocks offers a good spot for a picnic with a view.

The path continues, back over the black pipe, heading initially SSW/210 degrees. But a minute later, *do not follow the pipe down but follow the mini-cairn I have erected up to the right*, in a SE direction, steeply upwards. *Ignore a fork to the left*, instead make a 2' climb up to the right. Keep to the main path.

The laurel trees are by this point becoming more bearded with green moss. Within 10 minutes, a short detour to the left offers a view out. You continue straight on, following the black pipe. A couple of hundred metres later, still following the pipe, *you go up rocks to your right,* with the path up the rocks fairly clear. Ignore a fallen tree leading to the left, go up to the top following the pipe. After passing a concrete hatch into which the pipe runs, *you go up some more rocks.*

A very short way after the rocks, *it looks as if your path could continue to your right, but you follow the black pipe up to the left, scrambling up.* I have blocked off this false trail with small branches and put a mini-cairn on the rocks to your left, to indicate your way upwards (initially in a SSE/160 degrees direction). Your path onwards and upwards is obvious enough, initially SW/220 degrees, following the pipe.

The next rock face you come to is the highest. You can scramble up it any way you like (you need to get where the waterpipe goes) but the easiest way is to keep straight ahead just below the left edge of the rockface, and at the very far end of it, zig to the right and upwards, past a dead and forlorn small tree. After scrambling to the top, where there is another concrete hatch for the waterpipe, go towards the valley you have come from, and, in the right conditions, you have a magnificent view back towards Vallehermoso. You can then see a mini-cairn marking the continuation of your path, away from the view, initially in a SW direction.

Following the pipe, within five minutes you come to another concrete hatch. Soon, you can touch to your left hand side the greenest and hairiest tree of them (a dozen trunks growing out of the same spot). Shortly after this, you should be able to hear the first cars from the road ahead.

So within an hour and a half since beginning the climb from the reservoir wall – allowing for generous breaks – *you reach the tarmac road.*

Turn right along it (for those who are tired: if you look at the map you will see it is quicker to go left and then right along the main road to Las Hayas, missing out the easy and pleasant downhill stroll on routes 48 and 10). For those on the main walk: within 12 minutes or so, *you come to a very prominent road track below you to your left,* the **Camino Forestal Jardin de Las Creces**, signposted 'Las Hayas 3km'). Scramble down to this car road track, or go to its official entrance, and continue down through the laurel forest, and within 10 minutes *you come to a vast picnic site*, with water taps, tables and barbecue stoves.

Your trail continues off to the right, signposted 'Las Hayas 2.6', initially NW/305 degrees, away from the barbecue stoves – it has a chain across it, slung between two tree trunk pillars. The trail zigzags at long intervals. Keep on the main trail, *ignore a sign left saying 'Las Hayas 0.7'.* Soon you see buildings ahead on the far hillside, made of breeze blocks, with a concrete fence and with telegraph poles and cables between them running diagonally downhill. Your car road track becomes a trail. Keep due South and then bear right, soon on a path through the middle of the fields, your direction WSW/240 degrees, towards a house in the distance with a green fence to its right. (You can see the red car track ahead of you that you need, leading to this house.)

Going through the middle of the vineyards, you pick up this road track, and within 200 metres you come to the main road, and on the other side is the **Bar Montana**, which my cynical friend Bob describes as 'a rip-off, serving peasant food at non-peasant prices'. He hasn't appreciated that it is more theatre than food that one is paying for at the Bar Montana. Nevertheless, it is perhaps worth telling Dona Efigenia, the friendly and enterprising woman who runs the place, that 'es urgente' and that you have a long way still to 'caminare', as service is incredibly slow, however few the guests, with those serving you disappearing entirely for long periods. Meals are so huge that one year we ate our fill off other's leftovers, just whilst waiting for our drinks. There is also a small shop counter within the Bar. But beware: whatever food you ask for, you tend to get the same. We asked merely for a soup and got the usual 'Gomeran speciality' feast nevertheless – a huge vegetable soup with mountainous potatoes dumped in the centre, surrounded by beans and corn, plus 'gofio' maize paste like a hot porridge with a 'mojo' red sauce made of hot pepper, garlic and vinegar, and almond pudding with date treacle ('miel'). Normally there is a huge salad dish too. This, with coffee and generous quantities of Vino de Gomera, came to 1,500 pesetas each. One year, we got served, offered to pay as the last course was delivered, and got out in one hour 38 minutes, which we thought must be some kind of record – but in 2001, we ordered just wine and a bar of chocolate from the bar shop and were away in 15 minutes. But I love the whole slow food experience, and the room crowded with German walkers up from Valle Gran Rey. Some years, these have been the first other walkers we have met since starting out from San Sebastian, and the long tables with large bowls passed between guests helps create a very convivial feel, despite the cold. You can get the same Gomeran food, at ordinary prices, at Bar Sonia in Chipude, your evening destination, but without many tourist trappings.

Leaving the Bar Montana, you turn right and keep on the main road, coming to the first house on the right (Bar Amparo), where you *take the paving stone steps downwards to your right*, with the bar to your left hand side, heading Southwards, towards the house below with the flat orange roof.

By this house, the path you are joining is concreted, turn left along it, your direction ESE/105 direction, and continue straight on when the concrete ends, initially in a Easterly direction, beside palm trees. Here one year we met farmers out with their bullocks ploughing the fields, with a little calf following the bullocks wherever they went. *Carry on, ignoring turn-offs*, with the valley and palm trees on your right, then more upwards. Within 10 minutes of leaving Bar Montana, *you come to a house, and your path upwards is on the left hand side of this house. You cross a car road track and continue on a concreted footpath straight on. Within 2 minutes, take the left hand fork (your direction due South) going upwards.* Within 3 minutes of this fork, on your left hand side, there is a field of palm tree stumps. A minute later, *on the brow of the hill, you can see the village of El Cercado*, your interim destination, on the far hillside ahead of you, underneath Fortaleza table mountain (in a SSE/160 degrees direction). Behind El Cercado to its right is your final destination, Chipude. This is the point to decide whether to follow my suggested route, straight on, or to follow Alternative 3A below, which means turning right for the alluring juice bars and nudist beach of overcrowded Valle Gran Rey – where you may have difficulty finding accommodation, and where I always quickly regret coming down from the mountains to re-enter 'civilization' (although I have to admit that my companions never seem to pine for the hills to the same extent).

Day 3 Alternative A: from beyond Las Hayas to Valle Gran Rey

Toughness: 4. Beauty: 6. Hours: 3.

This is three hour walk mostly steeply downhill, and hard on the knees, by route 7 to Los Descansaderos. Be extra careful on damp days to ensure that each footfall grips on the rocks.

Having turned right, as above, keep the vertigo-inducing Barranco del Agua on your left, and soon you have a magnificent view of the Gran Rey valley, and your path onwards is clear, although narrow at points. Within ten minutes, you come to *a very steep descent down rocky steps*. In about an hour you come to a water aqueduct. Cross this, and continue on, with concreted steps down beside houses leading you onto the asphalted road at **Los Descansaderos**. Often taxis

N
Arguamal
Vallehermoso
Day 2 Walk
Day 8/3A Walk
Epina
Alojera
Day 3 Walk
Banda de las Rosas
Presa de Los Gallos
Tagaluche
Arure
Las Hayas
Los Descan-saderos
El Cercado
Day 10 Walk
Day 11/4A Walk
Alto de Garajona
Chipude
Day 11/4B Walk
Pavón
Ermita de los Reyes
Valle Gran Rey
Erque
Erquito
Imada
Day 4 Walk
El Drago
Alajero
La Manteca
Magaña
La Dama
Arguayoda
La Rajita
Day 5 Walk
Kilometres
0 1 2 3 4 5

La Gomera

Overview of Walks

(see German Golstadt Wanderkarte map for details)

- Day 2 Walk
- Agulo
- Lepe
- La Caleta
- Ermita de San Juan
- El Palmar
- Hermigua
- Casas de Juel
- ceviños
- Day 6 Walk
- El Cedro
- Casas de Encherada
- Lomo Fragoso
- Casas de Jaragan
- Ermita de Lourdes
- La Laja
- Day 1 Walk
- Alto de Garajonay
- Day 14/7A Walk
- Roque de Agandos
- Degollada de Peraza
- Benchijigua
- ada
- Azadoe
- San Sebastian
- Seima
- Day 13/6A Walk
- ajero
- Casas de Contrera
- El Cabrito
- Targa
- Day 12/5A Walk
- Day 5 Walk
- Santiago

◉ = Towns
● = Places with pensions or rooms
• = Hamlets (or less than)
▲ = Summit

deposit walkers at this spot, so you could wait for one, if tired by now, or thumb a lift to your right on the main road to Valle Gran Rey. If carrying on walking, instead *turn left on the road*. Keep going in a South Westerly direction along this road, ignoring any turn off right down into the riverbed, until a trail, rather than the road, keeps you going on in a South Westerly direction towards the **Ermita de los Reyes** (ask local people for the Ermita, if unsure of this track). The Ermita courtyard is where town festivals seem to take place, complete with bars and dancing. *Cross the courtyard and continue on the track, till you come to an industrial site on your left, at which point you can make your own way (right) down to the riverbed and up the other side, scrambling up to the main road and then, if you would like a brief but pleasant shortcut, up a little path that joins the La Calera road up into town.* If you miss the start of this path, simply backtrack uphill on the main road, and turn left onto the La Calera apshalted road.

Valle Gran Rey

Follow this La Calera road to the very end, straight on through town, and when it seems to end, find a narrower continuation slightly to the left. At the very end, with a view out over the sea and the banana plantations below, is my favourite haven, the **Bar Orchidea** (open 10am to 1pm and 5pm to 10pm, closed on Sundays), where you can sit under an avocado tree (even if the place is closed), listen to music from the vast array banked along the wall behind the bar, admire the bourgainvillea, befriend the cats, and wait in a stupor of beauty for the cool and timeless service provided by Jose Antonio (who might possibly be an ageing hippie with his curly long hair, balding on top). Controlling the apartments above the bar (tel 922 805030; the top apartments have their own breakfast terrace, and wonderful views) was **Senor Dominguez**, an elderly man with eye trouble. We encountered him in the bar, and asked if he had a room for one night only. He said No. We sat there for a while, chatting amiably, caught in the spell of the place and with no desire to move on – Bar Orchidea always reminds me of Circe's island that nearly ensnared Odysseus on his travels. I was busy helping Senor Dominguez's puppy attempt to befriend a kitten when Senor Dominguez relented and remembered that there was an apartment not reserved until tomorrow after all, at 5,000 pesetas for two people. (A younger Senora Dominguez now seems to be in charge of admin.)

Another year, we went next door to **Apartamentos Rivas** (5,500 pesetas for two people for one night, tel 922 805068). But if neither of these is available, you may have to begin the accommodation trek, asking everyone as you go, on the way that may lead you, if all else fails, in the direction of the town's port – out past the massive promenade scheme funded by the European Community. (Wherever you see inappropriate or unnecessary or grandiose schemes on the island, such as asphalted roads going nowhere at all, you can be sure it was dreamed up as a way of absorbing EC funds.)

A friend recommends **Villa Aurora** (tel 922 805053), run by Pedro, and situated in an old courtyard down towards the port, turn left after the banana plantations and go beyond the school.

Other guide books list the following (note that Vueltas is the port area, La Playa the beach, La Calera the main old road in town):

Ramon, La Calera (6 beds, tel 922 805672).

Las Jornadas, Playa La Calera (25 beds, tel 922 805047).

Las Vueltas, Vueltas (10 beds, tel 922 805216).

Casa Rudolfo, at the Playa (tel 922 805195).

The tourist board list the following other relatively inexpensive places (with the cheapest listed first):

Abraham, Vueltas (tel 922 805424).

America (tel 922 805462).

Celia, Las Vueltas (no phone).

Mendoza (tel 922 805446).

Montesinos, Ctra. del

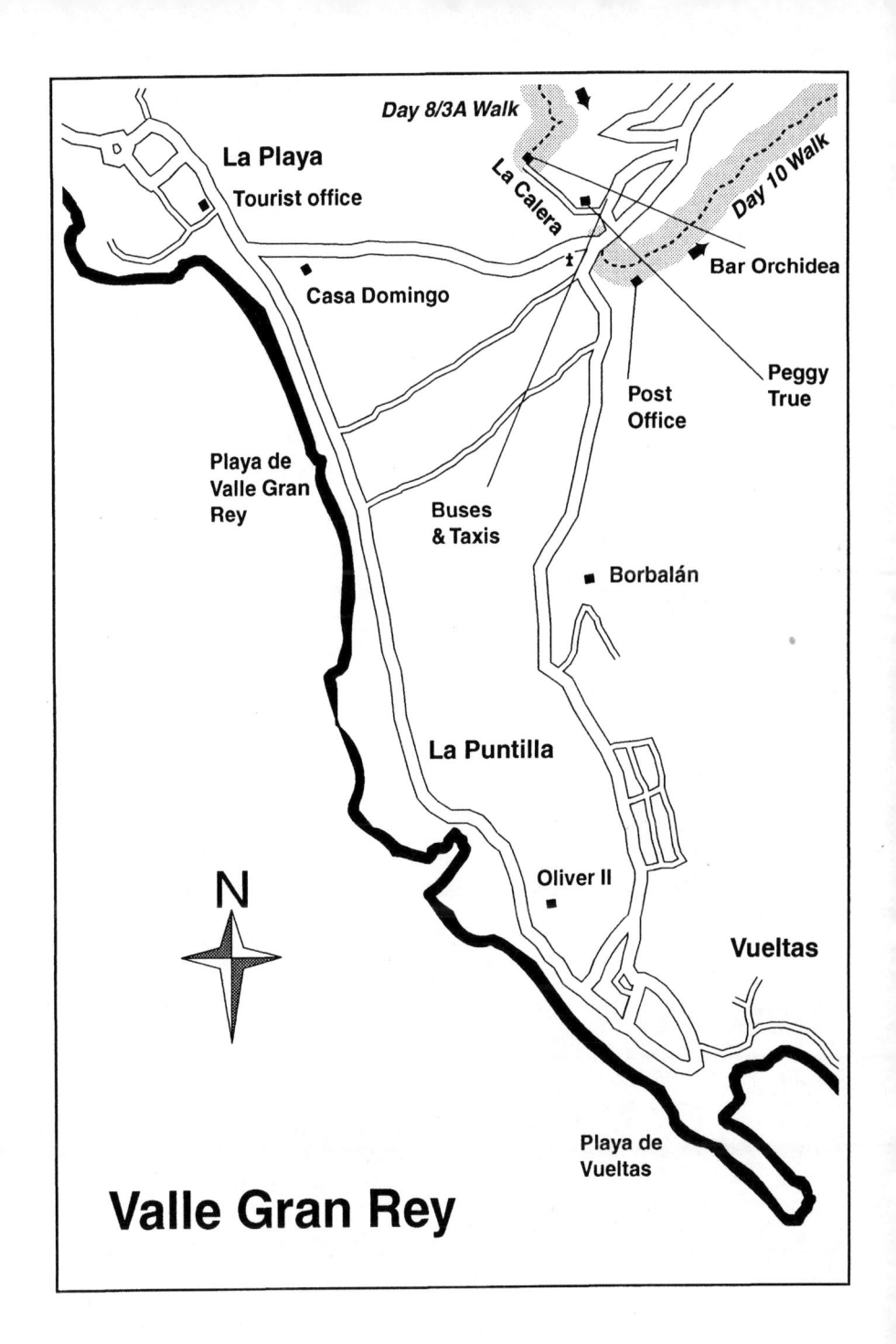

Valle Gran Rey

Puerto (tel 922 805048).
Yenay (tel 922 805471).
Damas, Vueltas (tel 922 805052).
Roni y Lu (tel 922 805015).
Jobel (tel 922 805425).
Casa Policarpo, El Chorro (tel 922 805143).
Eva, La Calera, sn (tel 922 805145).
Genara, C/Lepanto, La Playa (tel 922 805066).
Gran Rey, La Orijama (tel 922 805039).
El Molino (tel 922 287775).
Oliver II, Vueltas (tel 922 805337).
Oliver, Vueltas (tel 922 805153).
Vidal, Vueltas, sn (tel 922 805275).
Borbalan, Barrio Borbolan, sn Valle Gran Rey (no phone).
Bajio, La Puntilla (tel 922 805138).
Carlos, Lepanto (tel 922 805052).
Conchita, Las Orijamas (tel 922 805452).
Damas, La Orijama (tel 922 805428).
Ernesto, Las Orijamas (tel 922 805168).
El Garaje, La Pista (tel 922 805129).
Jornadas, Playa de la Calera (tel 922 805047).
Lili, Las Orijamas (tel 922 805081).
Los Naranjos, Las Orijamas (tel 922 805168).
Dos Palomera, La Palomera (tel 922 805129).
Puesta del Sol, C/Calera – El Ancon, sn (tel 922 805074).
Colon (tel 922 805402).
Avenida, Vueltas (tel 922 805461).
Berta, Vueltas (tel 922 805327).
Cabello, Vueltas (tel 922 805132).
Canario, Borbalan, sn (tel 922 805139).
El Chorro, La Calera, sn (tel 922 805077).
Senor Dominguez (another Senor Dominguez, not the one described above, tel 922 805181)
Elias, Vueltas, sn (tel 922 805185).
Iballa, Borbolan, sn (tel 922 805152)
Navarro, Vueltas (tel 922 805107).
Nelly, Canda de la Rosa (tel 922 805084).
Vista Mar (tel 922 805525).
Yamina, Pto. de Vueltas (no phone).

According to my companion Bob, the best place to sleep on the beach is at the **Playa des Ingles**. To get there you go to the seafront and turn right on a car track that leads to the beach about 400 metres past the last house. (The sea at this beach is dangerous, with hidden rocks and an undercurrent with every seventh wave – one woman drowned here on her honeymoon, another broke her arm; in February 2000, during our visit, a man drowned here.) You cannot camp on the black sandy (nudist) beach itself, but the police seem to turn a blind eye if you camp back from the beach on the left hand side of the road (there is a football stadium on the right hand side). At Easter time there can be about 50 people there, nearly all with tents. The so-called **Rainbow Beach** is depressing by comparison. For this you go left at the seafront to the second bay along. It is rocky and has large stones, and only one or two people camping there.

This Rainbow Beach is a rocky path onwards from the **Argayall new age centre,** with various new age therapies on offer, which is in the previous bay, the Playa de Argayall, a single story building with a garden, with entry by invitation only (tel 922 697008 between 10am and 12-30; rishi@Argayall.com; www.Argayall.com).

Trips out to see the **dolphins** (not to swim with them) are possible from Valle Gran Rey – phone Club de Mar (922 805 759 to reserve a place in a small boat outing). Indeed a UK outfit, Dolphin Connection (tel 01273 882778), offer holiday packages with dolphins as the main theme or 'transformation holidays' with therapies and dance plus dolphins.

Next day, or whenever you can drag yourself away, one pleasant way of climbing out of Valle Gran Rey is on route 3 to Chipude via El Cercado (see below for details), or, if you start early enough, you could get a lift to **Chipude** and join my suggested walk for Day 4.

There is a **bus** from Valle Gran Rey at (*= not Sunday or festival days) 5am*, 7.30am, 12.30pm*, 2pm, 4pm* to Arure, El Cercado, Las Hayas, Chipude,

Parajito, Degollada de Peraza and San Sebastian (it stops by the bottom of the Calera, having started 10 minutes earlier at the beach, and 5 minutes earlier at the port – Vueltas. It may be worth going to the beach as I have found that it is often full by the time it gets to the Calera). It takes 2 hours minutes to get to San Sebastian. A phone number for **taxis** in Valle Gran Rey is 922 805058.

The **health clinic**, with GP in attendance, is the Centro de Salud, in La Calera (tel 922 807005). The **tourist office**, Officina de Turismo, is at Calle Lepanto, s/n La Playa (tel 922 805458).

Day 10 Walk: Valle Gran Rey to Chipude via El Cercado

Toughness: 5. Beauty: 5. Hours: 6.

This day of walking follows the German map's route 3 to El Cercado; then my 'Day 3 continued' directions (see below) from El Cercado to Chipude. The way includes about 3 kilometres of a steep path up the barranco into El Cercado. Average walkers should reach El Cercado by the early afternoon; and then, allowing time to have lunch and to see the pottery workshops, you should reach Chipude in the late afternoon. Here are the details:

Starting in Valle Gran Rey from the taxi rank outside Bar Parada, go right. *Take the steps down opposite the Cepsa garage, down to the valley floor.* Then in 20 metres, *turn left on a stony car-wide track*, in 20 metres forking left now following up the valley floor, your direction NE/45 degrees, *parallel to the main road* to your left hand side.

In 125 metres, ignore a white circle and steps going up to your right. In a further 120 metres, ignore a right turn. Then in 150 metres, go under an overhead water pipe, your route following a line of pylons.

In 350 metres, you go under these pylons. Then in 75 metres, *fork left towards a long flat single storey building*, a hundred metres ahead of you, your direction NNE/30 degrees. 450 metres beyond this building, by a telegraph pole, ignore a fainter fork straight on, to *fork left*, your direction 154 degrees, *over the valley floor*, and pick up the car-wide track on the other side of the valley floor. *Fork right through a bamboo grove*, heading due East, still on a car-wide earth track.

In 300 metres, *turn right on the smaller path that crosses yours*, your direction ESE/120 degrees. You can see the cross of the Ermita above you to your right hand side. In 30 metres, you start going up steps towards this **Ermita de los Reyes**.

10 metres beyond the Ermita, fork right uphill on a path, your direction SE/130 degrees. In 35 metres, ignore a turn to the right. In a further 50 metres, pass a mini-dam to your right hand side. Then in 35 metres you pass a sign for the Parque Rural Valle Gran Rey. You are now high above the valley floor, but parallel to it.

In 140 metres, by white slashes on rocks, ignore a faint turn sharp right uphill. Keep on the main path, your direction 70 degrees.

In 90 metres, ignore another turn to the right, by a white slash on a rock.

Then in 20 metres, by a house with stones set in the white wall, and palm trees on your left hand side, ignore a way to right, to continue on downwards, bearing left.

In 400 metres, you come *to a road and turn left*, your general onward direction NE/55 degrees.

In 215 metres, ignore a way up to the right. In a further 40 metres, *fork right on the road going uphill*. In 25 metres, you pass Casa Eligio on your right hand side.

In 160 metres ignore well-made crazy paving steps up to your right. In a further 90 metres, ignore railings and a path going up to your right. Then in 135 metres, ignore a well-made crazy paving path going gently uphill.

In a further 50 metres, at a steep bend in the road to the right, *go left up crazy paving steps, a three storey house to your left hand side*. There is also a blue arrow marked 'Cerkado'.

In 100 metres, ignore a sharp turn downwards to your right. In 45 metres, *at* a T-junction, go right, upwards, your direction ESE/ 115 degrees. In 25 metres, *turn left on a tarmac road.*

In 30 metres, *take the concrete steps upwards, by a white lamppost.* In 65 metres, fork upwards on a paved stepped way, a red circle on the wall to your right hand side.

In 35 metres, ignore a turn to the right (a stepped way with railings).

In a further 80 metres, fork right, following red arrows and a red circle, still heading uphill.

In a further 200 metres, take the middle path upwards over rocks.

Then in 250 metres, *keep to the main path,* ignoring a faint turn-off to the right.

The route onwards and upwards is straightforward, and eventually, in over 2 kilometres, you can see El Cercado ahead. You come to a sign for the Parque Rural Valle Gran Rey and *to a T-junction. Turn left on a car-wide earth road.* In 30 metres, ignore a fork in the road to the right. In 70 metres, ignore a fork right by a telegraph pole. You come to the **Bar Maria** and **Bar Restaurante Victoria** in **El Cercado**, and continue, using the directions from the second paragraph below.

Day 3, continued, from beyond Las Hayas to Chipude

Toughness: 2. Beauty: 7. Hours: 2.

For those on the full Day 3 suggested walk: *Your trail is straight over, and on left-wards,* your direction ESE/ 120 degrees, towards the main asphalt road in the distance. *Keep on the main path* (so at the T-junction within three minutes, take the main path to the right). Your path heads seemingly down into the barranco. On the opposite side of the barranco you can already see your green zigzagging path that will take you up to Cercado. It is a wonderfully vertiginous route to look down if you are not overly affected by heights. Within 7 minutes of the fork to Valle Gran Rey, you come to a large water trough on the left of the path. You reach the pond and frogs at the bottom within 6 more minutes. *Going over the pool and upwards the other side,* you pass on your right an impressive skyline of rocks that looks somewhat like a submarine.

You cross over a second streambed and begin the ascent the other side, keeping to the main path all the way up. Within 8 minutes of this second stream you see a little house on the rim of the barranco above you. Head up towards a house with a tattered green fence beside it (thus turning right at the T-junction 200 metres below it). Within some 30 minutes of the earlier Valle Gran Rey fork, you are on the main road by the **Bar Maria** of **El Cercado**, and, turning right, in another 30 metres, you come to the **Bar Restaurante Victoria** run by Bernardo (tel 922 804146).

(If you detour a little further along the Cercado asphalt road, you come to the fascinating pottery workshops where you can watch the women at work. They use centuries-old Guanche techniques for making ceramics without a potter's wheel, hand-shaping and firing 'ollas' bowls out of reddish clay fetched from two barrancos away.)

Go down concreted steps to your right, opposite the Bar Restaurante Victoria, your direction ESE/125 degrees and follow a concreted path initially parallel to the right. *Go right at a T-junction* onto a paved road, your direction SSE/165 degrees. This turns into a tarmac road, and after 40 metres of tarmac, by a white lamppost and just past a blue garage door, *go left up a path,* due South. In 100 metres you rejoin the main road.

Cross the main road and continue uphill, following the lampposts, your direction SE/145 degrees. Skirt to the right of a house at the top. Cross an earth road and Chipude is ahead of you. You go down following a thin waterpipe to the asphalt road, and *straight over this main road, and on down the trail,* your direction Eastwards/85 degrees, over a stream and up the other side. *Turn right on the main road,* and you are in the outskirts of **Chipude**. *By the bus shelter, turn left up steps to its left hand side* then head left up a cobbled car road track (initially SE/140 degrees) for 35 metres, then *right up steps,* your direction SSW/205 degrees, into the centre of Chipude. At the top, turn left, towards the Chipude cemetery and the huge Chipude Church behind it. **Bar Sonia** is on the other side of the square from the church.

Day 3 Alternative B: Vallehermoso to Chipude (or Valle Gran Rey) via Arure

Toughness: 6 (not for vertigo sufferers). Beauty: 9. Hours: 11.

This is an alternative to the walk through Los Loros and the rainforest. It is less steep, but a slightly longer way round (about 22km). It does not take in so much of the laurel forest, has not got such a wild feel, but is almost equally attractive, if you should have extra time at some point in your stay on Gomera. It goes close to the cliff edge down by Arure, and is therefore not a walk for very windy days. Allow between 10 and 11 hours if going very slowly – and add up to 3 hours if stopping for an evening meal at Bar Montana on the way. A shorter 8 hour walk is to go on from Arure to Valle Gran Rey rather than Chipude. There are also several main roads that would shorten the walk along the way, and several places where you could drop out and get a lift, taxi or bus if you have had enough. Or you could possibly find a place to stay overnight in Alojera, Tagaluche, Arure or El Cercado – all villages that are near or on your path. The walk is brambly for a very short while up beyond the Choros de Epina bar and you may need leg protection of some kind.

The walk details in full are as follows: *head up the road next to **Vallehermoso's** Bar Central, away from the plaza. Almost immediately (after house No. 5) you turn left up some concrete steps. At the first turning to the right of these steps (going initially Northwards) you follow them up*, avoiding the path straight on. You can see the castellated side of the main road above you.

You come to this asphalt road and cross it – carrying on up more concrete steps – the left hand set which leads up parallel to the main road, and keeping to the leftwards.

The concrete comes to an end at the last house, painted white (and ochre below), and there is a three-way fork going on from it. *You take the middle, most upward fork*, initially Westwards, following a handmade sign to Epina. Where this path in 10 metres bends round to the right, you follow it round along the fence at the back of the house, with then almost immediately a view from the ridge to the sea on your right. You carry on with the same path, still heading Westwards.

Within 18 minutes of setting out, you pass a cemetery below you (rows of containers, not graves and crosses).

Within 4 minutes of this, and at the next sharp bend, with a conical needle of rock touchable ahead of you, stick to the main path on its left bend. You are now back looking down into Vallehermoso, and you follow your path, gently upwards, on its subsequent bends, as it heads up towards the top. Soon you have a view down both sides of the ridge. *Near the peak, you keep on the main path, through a pass* (with rocks up to your left to the summit and a ridge on your right) and you are then finally away from the Vallehermoso valley, your direction initially Westwards.

Your onward path is towards an electricity pylon in the distance. Keep to the main path as it zigzags up. Soon you are parallel to pylon cables below you (and 100 metres to your left) – and you remain parallel to them for quite some time.

Next there is a view of the sea behind you to the right. You cross under the pylon cables and you have a fine view to your left. In a while you can see to your right your next interim destination, a phone and TV transmission aerial with satellite dishes and a pylon beside it.

Keep on the main path (ignore a suggestion of a path to the right and uphill, 100 metres before the aerial). You come to a viewing platform (made by nature) with good views out over the barrancos.

Stay on the main path, and *it becomes a car track which in 20 metres joins an asphalt road, on which you go left and downwards*, your direction WSW/250 degrees. Slow walkers may have taken over one and a half hours to get to the top.

In 280 metres you come to a main road where the options are:

(1) going right, which leads to Alojera on an asphalt road, with beyond it a car track down to Playa de Alojera, where Miguel runs a fish restaurant and there are apartments.

(2) Going right and immediately right again leads to Arguamul, a car track all the way. Route 20 on the German map is a right fork taken later on along this track, and goes between Ermita Santa Clara and Buneavista – it is recommended as particularly beautiful in a stark way.

(3) This is your suggested route for the day. *Turn left onto this main road,* initially Southwards, and ignoring any tempting forks later.

Soon you come to a T-junction, with left going back to Vallehermoso and right towards Chipude and Valle Gran Rey. *You go right* (and on a clear day you can then see La Palma island to your NNW/340 degrees, and Epina village below you). *You come to* **Choros de Epina** *bar restaurant,* which had three coach loads of tourists arrive in the brief time we were there. The best way to get out quick seems to be to order whatever the coach parties are having and to pay as the food arrives.

If coming out of the restaurant, you turn right on the asphalt, and in 50 metres you come to a Parque Nacional sign and a sign to Choros de Epina.

Turn right down this crazy paving car track and in a couple of hundred metres you come to the **Ermita S. Isidro**.

Ignore the well-made steps down to the right just before the Ermita. *Pass by the Ermita on its left side and your path continues straight on,* a narrow path initially WSW/245 degrees, and one that in the past has been a bit brambly and overgrown (it was fine in 2001). You may need leg protection for this. A small reservoir is immediately below you to your NE. Ignore a fork off to the right (by '33X' in red paint on a cairn) and keep to the main path (passing a cairn marked 'X32') with the valley of Epina on your right. You are soon passing through one of the few pasture-like lands of the island.

You come to the reservoir seen from above and you go along the left edge of it. There is a post to say Monumento Natural Lomo del Carréton. You can see Alojera to your West by the sea and an enormous extraordinary plastic-sided reservoir above it. *You go straight on,* despite the fact that the most used path turns right at the far end of the reservoir, and another faint track goes off uphill. You are heading towards Alojera. *Your path is downhill to the main road below, weaving in and out of the line of telegraph poles below you.* If the path is not well-defined to begin with, *head down to the 2 metres wide drystone wall roofless shelter below you,* at which point the path becomes better defined and broader, its onward continuation below to the WSW/260 degrees also being evident.

Keep heading down, ignoring any turn-offs, and still going in and out of the telegraph poles.

You come out on the main road, close to the telephone cable, which is still to your right. The exit is marked by a post with another sign for Lomo del Carréton.

It is now up to about 3 hours since setting out.

You turn left at this main road. Within half a kilometre (8 minutes) of doing so, you take a fork left (initially SSE/160 degrees) signposted to Tageluche. You remain on this road for two and a half kilometres, and you therefore do not need to concern yourself about any turning-offs from your road until such time as your road has passed half a kilometre beyond a 90 degrees bend to the right

After about 45 minutes of being on this road, you cross under a pylon cable, with the pylon just above and 20 metres to your left hand side. At this point, take note of the summit crag on your road ahead to your WNW/290 degrees (after the bend to the right) – it forms the top right of the skyline ahead. It is by this summit that you will need to turn left up a path.

The sharp right hand bend ahead on your road is now evident. Ignore three tracks off to the left (yours will be well marked when it comes). You pass under the pylon cables again, and a pylon is up above you, 80 metres to your SW. Ignore another faint path up to the left.

At the hairpin bend in the road, a Monumento Natural Lomo del Carréton sign marks the entry to your path upwards, initially in a Southwards direction, and very clearly defined. The outskirts of **Alojera** are below you and a path going downwards towards the town heads off to your East. (If you happen to come up this path from Alojera, keep to the right. Note that there is a very dangerous undertow on the beach at Alojera.)

Your path is steeply upwards, and soon parallel to the road below and heading for the pylon that you were walking below earlier. *Within 5 minutes of starting this path, ignore the path off to the right,* and keep on for the pylon, now 80 metres away. 40 metres past the pylon, you go left, your direction East/85 degrees, then in 100 metres there is a fork, with either way coming to the same point. *Then stay on the main path, ever upwards, heading to the left of the crag near the top.* You go in a vaguely Southerly direction, except very near the top where you need to bend leftwards for a while with the main path away from the Arure destination, to get around the crag.

Next, the island of Hiero may be visible to your WSW/260 degrees, and the village of Tagaluche is below you in the same direction.

You pass striated vertical columns of rock on your left, like a giant's tipped-over piano keys.

Your path is level enough, the view stunning, the drop vertical, the path narrow and the wind, I hope, weak. Watch your feet and hold on to your hat.

You pass through laurel trees and you will see two submarine-like rocks to your SSW/200 degrees, above a main road parapet and a terrace (of the Ermita) where your path ends.

You pass under more larch trees, past a little red mini-cave with a white chalk ceiling where brave travellers have slept. Beyond a red seam of rock on your left, the very evident path right to **Tagaluche** heads down, initially NNE/20 degrees. There is another Ermita visible there (one where families go to have barbecues).

Your onward path is past the Ermita de Santa ahead of you (much construction was going on under this in 2001, probably either a cafe or car parking or a mirador) and go left under the bridge, and down to the car road. You are probably within five and a half hours of setting out.

Ahead of you is **Arure**. First right, initially Southwards, on the small tarmac car road, leads to Valle Gran Rey, as follows. (For those heading for Chipude, see further on.)

Arure to Valle Gran Rey

After a couple of hundred metres on this car road, it bends right up towards a crag. Stay on this car track ignoring a wide trail off to the left going SW/220 degrees. You have a steep view down to Tagaluche on your right, soon with a concrete parapet wall on the right of your roadside.

Past 20 or so beehives on your left, you come to a plateau-like area. *At a fork in the road, don't go West and right, go left, SW/220 degrees, towards a peak* with its own row of trees, prominent on the skyline, leading up to it. Your route is to the left of the summit.

You come to steps going up to the right, SSW/195 degrees, with an arrow and 'VGR' on the rock. Go up these steep steps, leaving the car track, and a couple of minutes later crossing over a derelict water aqueduct. Soon you have a view down into Valle Gran Rey and the port. You go past a big cave for goats on the right hand side. Keep to the wide path (ignoring turn-offs) past drystone ruins on the left. Within 25 minutes of leaving the car track, the descent into Valle Gran Rey begins. Ignore a turn off to the right some 40 to 50 minutes later. If heading for Bar Orchidea in La Calera, you may like to try a short-cut: as you approach the buildings of Valle Gran Rey, *look out for a wide metal waterpipe heading off your trail to the right, and follow the almost non-existent path the pipe lies on,* over the brow towards the ocean. Bar Orchidea is the furthest right and lowest down building below you (beyond the brow, overlooking the sea, with several dustbin-like water containers on the roof). Weave your way down towards it, leftwards, down to La Calera, the mini high street, then right along this street to the very end.

Arure to Chipude

Incidentally, you can catch a bus in **Arure** leaving at (*= not Sunday or festival days) 10.10am* and 6.40pm for Valle Gran Rey; or one to San Sebastian (via Las Hayas, El Cercado and Chipude) leaving at 5.20am*, 7.50am, 12.50pm*, 2.20pm and 4.20pm*.

For this walk, you don't go right to Valle Gran Rey, as above, but *you go left (more or less straight on) on a small tarmac road leading in 125 metres to the more main road where you turn right*. In 190 metres, you pass a turning to the left to Ermita Virgen de la Salud.

(Now before you come to the next turning, you may see an unofficial shortcut path up the bank to your left to the tarmac road above you – a road that goes off to the left. If not:) 15 *metres before the shrine*, with the signpost offering Valle Gran Rey and Arure, you want neither of these, and *you will be turning left sharply*, heading initially ENE/70 degrees, uphill, on the tarmac road, signposted Las Hayas, El Carceda and Chipude.

You pass immediately under a telegraph cable that goes down over the chapel to your left.

You can keep on this main road to Las Hayas and Chipude, if pressed for time. If not pressed for time, in 180 metres, *just before the reservoir, turn off left* (for a scenic diversion on German map route 10) *down cobbled steps heading immediately below the walls of the reservoir* (marked simply as Embalse on the German map) *then right along the side of the reservoir*. You pass a white street lamp (and concrete steps up to your left) and *continue to the last house and its terrace, and then turn left near the side of the building and follow mini-cairns and a path, your direction NE/40 degrees*. Persevere onwards, towards the right hand end of Arure village, *within 50 metres your way comes to a main footpath and you turn along it to the right*, in a direction that is initially ENE/70 degrees.

Keep on this main path, go under pylons and carry on towards the wall of the reservoir Embalse de Arure (marked on the German map), your direction NE/45 degrees. In 600 metres *go left over the reservoir wall* of the **Embalse de Arure** – you are probably within 20 minutes of the previous large reservoir where this route 10 began.

On the far side, turn right and continue with the reservoir to your right hand side. You are now on a small tarmac road called '**Forestal a Las Hayas**' on the German map. *You will come to many left forks, but, for as long as the route is car-wide, always keep to the right fork (except the second fork right, a very sharp one heading due West, which you ignore)*. Your path is predominantly SSE/160 degrees.

Within 20 minutes of this last reservoir, just after another left fork, and with vineyards on both sides, your broad car-sized track becomes more just a well-defined trail, heading up a rocky path, your direction SE/145 degrees, with a terrace on your left, and, soon, earth steps up. The path winds up and up. Within 12 minutes of starting on this narrower trail, having been able to peer out below you to your left to a building and three sheds, *you come to a T-junction, and continue to your left*, ESE/100 degrees initially. Soon you are parallel to telegraph poles on your left hand side. *Ignore a turn-off to the left and keep with the poles*.

Within 5 minutes of these poles beginning, if you go up the 2 metre embankment on your left, from the top you can see Las Hayas to your SSE/160 degrees, and Fortaleza table mountain behind it. Ignore an asphalted turn sharply back to the right. *Go up between vineyards and fields and out onto the main asphalt road. Turn left and immediately uphill. On the other side of the road is the Bar Montana*. For your onward path from there to Chipude see the main Day 3 walk. One year, I chose to risk it and stay for the main dinner sitting at Bar Montana. Beware that this starts at 8.15pm and takes three hours and costs 1200 pesetas. I made a public appeal in German and English for an onward lift to Chipude but ended up walking most of the way there by torchlight. There were very few cars and it was cold, even in March. But the companionship and good food of Bar Montana were worth the after-dinner ordeal.

Chipude

Bar Sonia (tel 922 804158, run by Victor, his parents and his sister Sonia) seems to be the only place to stay in Chipude nowadays (rooms are 4,000 pesetas for two people for one night). We eat there too, although it is very cold, as these hardy but friendly folk tend to leave the front doors open. Two teenagers in this bar demonstrated 'el silbo' whistling language to me. One was saying to the other, 'go get yourself injected'.

Chipude has four bars (the **Bar Navorro**, tel 922 804132, next to the Bar Sonia, now has a supermarket where it used to have a restaurant, and no longer does accommodation – Bar Sonia seems to be winning the competition on all fronts).

Chipude is the highest village on the island at over 1,000 metres and can be very windy and cold. The times I have been there I've needed longjohns and all my clothes just to sit in the Bar Sonia restaurant since they always keep the doors open.

You may want to plan for Day 4 now – so see the note below at the start of Day 4, about phoning the pension in Alajero to book, as you may want to set out from Chipude too early the next morning to delay your call till then.

You can catch a **bus** in Chipude towards Valle Gran Rey (via El Cercado, Las Hayas and Arure) (*= not Sunday or festival days) at 11.45am, 3.15pm* and 6.45pm, 10.45pm; or a bus towards San Sebastian (via Pajarito) at 5.45am*, 8.15am, 1.15pm*, 2.45pm or 4.45pm*.

By the way, if you want an excursion to the top of Forteleza table mountain, something I've never had time for yet, Nick Holborne writes that 'it can be reached easily from Chipude by walking down the road to Pavon and heading up a broad footpath on the left. There is a short, very steep, section of path near the top, which is really more of a climb. A group of Germans behind us simply dumped their rucksacks in a heap before attempting it. There is a nice way back up the ridge to the *casa foresta*, then taking a left just after you enter the forest (on route 15). The whole thing should not take more than four hours.'

Day 4: Chipude to Alajero

Toughness: 10 (not for vertigo sufferers). Beauty: 10. Hours: 10.

We have never yet had a problem, even at Easter time, but it might be sensible to plan for this walk's destination pension in advance, by phoning Pension Villaverde in Alajero, and speaking with Hilde Villaverde (tel 922 895162) since hers is the only place to stay in town that I have been able to find, and if she is full, you might want to do the Chipude to Hermigua walk instead (the Day 4 Alternative A walk along route 15's Northern branch to Pajarito), followed by the main Day 6 walk, route 28, perhaps up to 10 hours in all, then the Day 3 Alternative via Arure and back to Chipude; ready to try again for Alajero – in which case, it might be sensible to book up Hilde now for the third and fourth night ahead (for if you have the time, this guide suggests booking for two nights in Alajero). If you prefer to chance your luck, be prepared to take a taxi on to Santiago or back to Chipude if Pension Villaverde is full (and if the hotel is still not finished).

The main suggested Day 4 walk is down route 16 to Erque and El Drago, then on a route South Eastwards to join route 57 to Alajero. The walk passes some of my favourite places on the island, past abandoned houses and hamlets I would love to be able to buy or to help renovate. The walk is 19 kilometres or so but is by far the toughest (but to me loveliest) walk so far, with many a barranco to climb up and down. You will probably know by now whether you have the endurance for it. Only attempt the full walk if all the walks until now have been well within your capacity, and if you have found following the walk directions relatively easy. There is a very steep descent from Fortaleza table top mountain at the start of the day that means going down rocks, sometimes in half metre steps, on paths that are not well-defined, although I have marked them at several places with mini-cairns, and my guidance is as detailed as I can make it. This steep descent would not suit those with huge packs on their backs (one option well worth considering for this particular walk is to send your pack ahead to the pension by taxi). Allow 11 hours if you have discovered by now that you are as slow as the times in this guide. Even the fastest walkers would take at least 6 hours, I think, allowing for short breaks.

You can shorten the walk in several ways, either by aborting it when tired, by taking one of the recently asphalted but still very traffic-free roads back up to the highway, from either Erque (this is where my companion Bob dropped out – the first part of the walk is a tough descent, with hard route finding, and we had been dramatically lost for hours previously) or El Drago (as described above, at the end of the section on Valle Gran Rey). Or you could start the day with a 10 kilometre lift along the road to Alajero, to the turn-off (right) to El Drago (a taxi could take you all the way to El Drago); then from El Drago rejoin the walk as described below. If you can only do part of the walk, the second half from El Drago is the easier and just as magical.

Whilst researching this route for the guide, Bob and I went entirely the wrong way near the outset, walked to within a kilometre or two of Alajero and had to hitch back to start again at about lunchtime. However, in retrospect, this way we found when lost seems to me to make the most pleasant of the possible alternative walks for those wanting a half-day walk into Alajero, and it is described below as Day 4 Alternative B. Anyway, we set out again after lunch to do the full walk, and despite getting lost many times more, and having to mark the right route with cairns, and having to write my notes, I finished the walk by 9pm. I ran down one barranco in the dusk and waited at the bottom of the next, lost, for the moon to rise. These are all risks that I strongly advise against – leaving my companion, going on alone, not having a torch (I forgot to ask him for it) and not expecting to finish before sundown.

The hamlets shown on the map for this day's walk are insubstantial or semi-abandoned in reality – although there were two locals who seemed 'mentally or alcohol challenged' in a house in Erque offering us beer but no water, and a house in El Drago gave me water. You could also abort the walk by going to Arguayoda if necessary, which has the pretence of a shop and bar, and continuing on to La Rajita, then up the steep cliff to La Dama, where, when I last visited, local people told me that there was at least one habitacion for rent – or a taxi can be phoned for. Traffic on the unasphalted roads from Erque and El Drago is very rare indeed.

Day 4 Alternative A: Chipude to Pararito, via Garajonay summit

Toughness: 6. Beauty: 4. Hours: 3.

This walk of about 3 hours (at a leisurely pace, and with time at the summit) is steadily uphill, is much frequented, and towards the end is a fairly dull trudge up a car track, with lots of other tourists. It is perhaps only worth doing on a very clear day, to take advantage of the views from the summit at Garajonay, which at 1486 metres is the highest on the island. The walk comes out at the start of Day 6's route 28, so you could connect with that, for a long day's walk in all, down into Hermigua.

The start described here may be very slightly different from that on some editions of the German map but is simple to follow: *As if coming out of Bar Sonia, turn right, to Bar Tito, then turn left, up a cobbled street,* in a NNW/340 degrees direction initially, *and then immediately right up another street* (your direction initially ENE/70 degrees), following telegraph poles and white street lamps upwards and towards an electricity substation. Keep on the cobbled path up, ignoring turn-offs. The path is soon an earth car track.

At the top, within 10 minutes of setting off, a waterpipe joins your path from your left hand side, and a (chained) car track from behind on your right hand side.

In a further 40 metres, a car track comes in from behind you on the left.

Within a couple of minutes *you come to an asphalted junction* where going right heads down to the main road. *You go left*, initially ENE/ 70 degrees, *up to a stone terrace* in 40 metres. Here you ignore the main fork left on a car road (initially NNW/ 340 degrees) and *go right*, your direction 85 degrees, *on a gravelled path*. In about 5 minutes, you ignore a main earth car track to the right (its direction SW/225 degrees) and continue straight on upwards, on a narrower path, your direction ESE/ 110 degrees. Within a further 10 minutes, *you come to a bent T-junction*. Ignore the way to the right down to the main road and *go left*, your direction 80 degrees, soon passing vineyards with wire mesh fence to your left hand side. Ignore a left fork downhill at the end of the vineyard. At the four-way crossing, go straight on towards 'Alto de Garojonay (2.3)' through a chain barrier.

Within 30 metres of this barrier, there is *a three-way fork. Take the one to the right*, the widest, signposted 'Alto de Garajonay', your direction initially SSE/160 degrees.

You come *to another bent T-junction*, and ignore the fork right downhill (SSE/ 160 degrees) and instead *fork left gently uphill*, your direction ESE/115 degrees, soon curving round to the right and upwards. At the next (signposted) fork, go straight on downhill, ignoring a way to the right (which goes off in the direction W/280 degrees).

In 150 metres, *go through a chain barrier and fork right uphill*, signposted 'Alto de Garajonay, 0.5', your direction SW/230 degrees. *In 15 metres, a pleasant short-cut to the summit is to fork left uphill* on a tiny path, your direction 190 degrees. In 40 metres, *at a crossing [*], turn right up log steps*, signposted 'Alto de Garajonay', steeply up to the summit.

At the top there is a rather cute house with garden, roofed with aerials, and above the house is a *drystone-style viewing circle*, with a pillar in the middle, which you can stand on to feel monarch of all you survey. You have reached the **Alto de Garajonay** and it is now within one and a half hours of setting off from Chipude. On the days I have been on the summit, it has been too cloudy to see the sometimes-visible islands of Tenerife (ENE/70 degrees), La Palma (NNW/340 degrees), Hierro (SW/225 degrees) and Gran Canaria (ESE/110 degrees). But I could see Fortaleza table mountain (W), El Cercado village (WNW), the outskirts of Hermigua (NE), pear-shaped Rock Agando (ESE) and La Dama (WSW).

To go down from the **summit** to Contradero: *Come back down to this crossing [* two paras above] but then carry straight on upwards*, your direction ENE/ 70 degrees. Ignore the next fork right and carry straight on, signposted 'Contradero'. Soon the path leads down onto a car-wide track where you go right downhill, your direction N/350 degrees. In due course you come down to the asphalted road and **El Contradero**.

The Day 6 walk starts on the other side of the road, slightly to your left (and is signposted El Cedro).

If going to the El Pajarito crossroads, turn right. There you have perhaps the best chance of a lift, once you are on your preferred onward road.

Start of both the Day 4 walk and the Day 4 Alternative B walk, from Chipude to Apartadero

Toughness: 2. Beauty: 6. Hours: 0.5.

For those doing either the full walk or Day 4 Alternative B walk, the start is the same: As if coming out of the Bar Sonia, *turn right out of the village, past the Bar Tito. Once out of the village, turn off left up a wide cobbled track heading Southwards/ 150 degrees initially* (as an alternative to the hairpin main road, which would do just as well for those who don't mind main roads as much as I do). The route is alongside the left hand breeze block side of a house which is also an unmarked bar, and may have crates outside. *You go uphill following the line of street lamps, cross the main road, and then on an earth trail down the other side, arriving within a couple of minutes back on the main road. Turn left. Almost immediately (in 30 metres) turn off it again and continue uphill*, heading SSE/ 170 degrees initially. (The just legible village sign on the main road below says Apartadero.) At the top there is house No. 31 with its varnished balconies and you go down the other side. *Just before the main road (where on your right is a petrol station and bar), you turn left up a cobbled path*, your direction ESE/100 degrees, *and go up, paralleling the main road on your right* (and avoiding the fork to your left). *Back down on the main road, you turn left along this to the Bar Los Carmioneros*, which is where the two walks separate.

Day 4 Alternative B: half-day walk from Apartadero to Alajero

Toughness: 4. Beauty: 8.
Hours: 4.

For the pleasant half-day walk: *just past the bar, fork left, off the main road, up a car road track in a direction that is initially NNE/60 degrees. Do not bend with the road back again, but go straight on to the left of the breeze block house and upwards, and then along the top edge of the cactus beds ahead. Beyond the cacti, you pick up a clear trail going out between two palm trees, heading NE. Now you join a better defined path, and carry on to your right between terraces on the left and rocks on the right* (and beyond the rocks for a time there is a wire netting fence). You join a large water pipe following your path on the left of you, and, briefly, a line of telegraph poles. You are heading ESE/110 degrees and up, still with the waterpipe. Within 6 minutes of first seeing the waterpipe, you cross over it, near the top, and *you cross a car road track at the top* (with a concrete roofed reservoir some distance away on your right). *Head straight across the road and down*, initially ESE/110 degrees. *At the end of the track, you come down onto a proper car road track heading in the same direction as yours* (indeed parallel to yours for 100 metres before you go down to it on your right).

This road track heads initially NE. At this stage you can see the distant loop to the right around the barranco, a route that you are destined to take.

As you do this loop round, a reservoir, down to your right in the valley below, reveals itself. At the first sharp bend in the road, *you can see a footpath zigzagging up to the left of you, initially WSW/ 250 degrees (marked with red and green dots and minicairn). Take this path.*

Once on the top, there is a fine view of Fortaleza table mountain to your WSW/ 260 degrees. Soon there is a pylon on your right. There is a hamlet flanked by terraces below you in the valley. La Dama is visible way off on a cliff above the sea. The Igualero Mirador viewpoint is ahead on the skyline.

You come to a stream with pools in the rock. Cross over. You come up to a pylon, whose nearest companion across the barranco you passed 10 minutes earlier.

You have pine forests on your left. Go on up to the next pylon (your third), getting to that within 8 minutes of the last. *You top a ridge within 5 minutes* – this marks the end of this particular mini-barranco, and the beginning of the next – *it has an area of red earth across the path.* Ignore a turn direct left alongside three pylons going up the mountain. *Go straight on, and bear to the left, and you will come to dilapidated terraces. You can see your continuing path on the opposite barranco side.*

Carry on along the main path to cross the streambed and continue on, your direction SSW/210 degrees.

Proceed on through a momentarily overgrown path past two more triangle signs. The path is ill-defined but heads towards the lowest pylon visible ahead, past another hunting sign saying more fully 'Zona de Reserva. Prohibido la Caza'. Your path improves slightly. Another 'Reserva de Caza' is to be seen on a flat rock. You go past a stone wall on the left of the path (an old goat pen?). Keep on the main trail under a pylon cable. You can see La Dama to the WSW/260 degrees, and Fortaleza table top mountain to the NW. *Soon you scramble down terraces onto the main asphalted road visible below. Walk or get a lift to Alajero to your right*, four kilometres away. *On the outskirts of Alajero, ignore a first sign saying Alajero Casco to your right.* You come to a rusty yellow VW displayed on a roof by the road side on your left. Then in 50 metres *there is a turn off to Alajero to your right. Don't take it.* In about 600 metres, by the first palm tree on your right as you come downhill, *turn sharp right onto a car track, initially NW, and then immediately, after 20 metres, left and down to the streambed and across towards the first substantial house on the hillside opposite.* This is Alajero's Pension Villaverde.

Day 4, full walk, continued, from Apartadero to Alajero

Toughness: 10 (not for vertigo sufferers). Beauty: 10. Hours: 9.5.

As if coming out of the Bar Los Camioneros, turn left and continue on the main road into the next hamlet, Pavon. You come to a white electricity sub-station, which the pylons feed out from. Turn left 30 metres beyond this, and go up a track beside a white house. Go up in a SSE/160 degrees direction initially, through the dilapidated hamlet of Pavon, on the main track upwards, ignoring turn-offs. The next hour includes some quite tricky route-finding, so it is worth being extra careful: Near the top, you come to the beginning of a field surrounded by a metal fence on your left; 20 metres after the start of this fence, *go right towards a Parque signpost. Veer left upwards and to the left of this Parque sign for 10 metres, your direction SSW/200 degrees*, and see a roofless outhouse below you and further ahead, also on the edge of the barranco, two stone houses about 30 metres apart. *Your route down is just below the far house* – to double check: this is a house which has the remains of a corrugated iron roof, a green door and no windows, and is below Fortaleza table mountain. Go the 50 metres towards this house (your direction SSW/210 degrees) and *take the path downwards below the house's front terrace*, the house now to your right hand side, a direction that is initially SW/225 degrees, very steeply into the barranco.

Within two minutes of this turn, you take big steps down, which are not wildly well-defined, but there is only one way, *straight down into the barranco.* (If you have a sense of alternative paths, keep to the right hand one.)

Within 8 minutes, when *you come to a patch of cactus* (if you were to press on through it, on what seems to be your straight-ahead path, it would become continually more impossible and prickly for your legs, as I know to my cost) and *your path goes down a ledge or little staircase or chimney of rock on your left, with steps in it made of placed stones, just before this cactus patch, going down about 10 metres*, and it proves easier than it looks (at least without a huge pack on your back). Your path then continues to your left, your direction NE/55 degrees. *Within 70 metres of this rock-staircase, you come to a junction of sorts, both trails going in a similar direction. You want the one two metres below, down a rocky scramble.* Your path onwards is thus initially ESE/110 degrees, in the direction of a village high up on the hillside ahead, and in the direction of the Igualero Mirador viewpoint (a roof suspended on columns) on the furthest horizon hilltop.

More mini-cairns indicate the straight-on path. After 80 metres of going on downwards, at the fork where there is a mini-cairn placed on top on the rock in front of you, do not continue left (WSW/250 degrees) horizontally, but bend down, initially SSW/ 205 degrees, and then on down. You are now looking down a promontory or long ridge of rock, with a way not very clearly defined, but it is easy enough to proceed on downwards, taking quite big steps down. There are no doubt a number of ways down, but it is easiest to tend to the left, and to keep to the rocks. Your direction is now SSE/160 degrees. Your interim destination is the streambed visible at the bottom of the valley below you (with a large rocky streambed to the right of it). Your path goes slightly to the left of the promontory's end point. I have put a number of mini-cairns to mark the way. It is still more of a scramble down over rocks than an easily recognisable path, but occasional rocks arranged as steps are a reassurance. *You head down towards the palm trees* (within 20 minutes of leaving the horizontal path and starting the promontory descent).

For a few metres at least it becomes a proper mini-footpath again, then off down on rock on a sort of path, still *heading down in the direction of the tiny reservoir.* It becomes quite steeply down. Head towards the nearest (and quite large) date palm. About 20 metres before getting to it (it turns out to be two palm trees next to each other) your path zigzags to the left and down (for the first 10 metres of the 'zig' it is Eastwards). I have put a mini-cairn to mark this. Then continue on without detours, onto a patch of trail where the way is not immediately clear, but it is still a matter of going straight on down. Again, I have put a number of mini-cairns to help make this clear. Soon, you can see your way down (a bit of a scramble this) to the well-defined path past the mini-reservoir below. You are soon down amongst the first of the group of palm trees. *You are soon in sight of the pools and streambed on your left, and just before the crossing your way towards it is to the leftwards away from the crossing point.* You are now within an hour and a half of starting your descent from Fortaleza and the worst is over.

Your path, once beyond the streambed, is very visible from above: onwards in a SSW/210 degrees direction, initially following along above the streambed, keeping to the main path, across two miniature water pipes (these within 3 minutes of crossing the streambed).

Almost immediately you see signs of houses ahead in the distance and your path now bends away from the streambed in an ESE/110 degrees direction, and you can see the houses more clearly – three joined together and an outhouse. You go over a rock outcrop and follow the main path upwards into a hamlet, the outskirts of **Erque** (ignoring a fork off down to your right.) You may like to find a big stick before going uphill, as the house at the top, Villa Garcia, had a fierce dog and inhabitants who were prepared to offer beer but not water. This could be your last opportunity for liquids till El Drago so it could just be worth accepting, if like me you travel with only half a litre of water. Your onward path is to the left of this house (marked Villa Garcia), and then you head down from it to the left, initially ENE/65 degrees. *You can see across the valley on the far hillside (SE/120 degrees) your onward path to the right,* the topmost of two horizontal paths – this, towards its right end, goes diagonally upwards to a telegraph pole marking your way out of the barranco, at the very top on the right hand side of the skyline. *Study carefully where you may have to join this path way down below, it is not so easy to find close up.*

Meanwhile, your path onwards is for the time being well-defined. You continue on up, to the left of the houses you see ahead. Two strange large nature-formed rock statues are on your right now – does it look like a huge dog lying down with a small lion next to it?

(At this point if you want to drop out and find your way back on the car road track from Erque, continue on up to the left of the palm trees, Northwards, and up to a house with palm trees.

Keep the house to your right. Ignore diversions off. Above the level of this house, your path bends right towards a second house, one with blue doors and a tall telegraph pool. Generally keep on upwards and leftwards wherever there is a choice, and you will come to a car-parking place – a good look-out point is marked on the German map, so you could have a chance of a lift from here, with patience. You can take the car road track in a North Westerly direction all the way to the main road, and hitch to Alajero – to your right once you get to the main road. Or you could look out for a green arrow on a rock and take the path to the right which is part of the Day 4 Alternative A described above, the one that comes out four kilometres North of Alojera.)

For those on the main walk: *Go down to the right, almost all the way to the stone 'statues', and all the way to the telegraph pole on their left.* From this, orient yourself so you walk NE and pick up the path towards the next pole. *15 metres before this second pole, keep right with the path as it goes lower,* your direction Eastwards/105 degrees, *heading for a clump of palm trees.* Once past these, the path goes between tall terraces, your direction ENE/70 degrees and you follow it till it bends abruptly downwards to your right, your direction now Southwards/190 degrees. *At the bottom, make you way over the streamed below the waterfall. Within 10 metres, you see a pair of dead but spiky trees on the left hand side. You push your way round the far edge of the last tree to the left* (anyone with an army knife please help cut back the growth here), *in a direction that is initially Eastwards. Keep on up and to the left of a huge boulder, and above it your very evident path (the one you saw from the opposite hillside) continues off to the right,* heading initially SSW/205 degrees. There may be a more elegant way to come to this path, but I have always been unable to find it.

Soon you see ahead of you the telegraph pole at the very top of the barranco (to your SE).

Your path is overgrown a bit with cactus and plants, but keep to this upper path, following the telegraph poles. Your direction is Southerly and so you pass and into the next barranco. You are at this stage within about 25 minutes of leaving the strange stone statues of Erque.

Soon you can see the village of Erquito, your next interim destination, below you to your South. At the top you are standing on a promontory of rock that extends off to your right and to another strange natural 'statue' – a huge lying-down horse, perhaps? If you make sure that you are at the bottom left edge of this promontory, you will see your faint onward path marked with a mini-cairn on its left. The path almost immediately curves left, going up to the left, initially in a NE direction. Avoid the temptation to head downwards to the hamlet below. *Head roughly towards the highest visible telegraph pole* (a newish one, made of light brown wood) your direction Eastwards/ 85 degrees. *Then at the first suggestion of a fork, head down towards this pole,* at which point your path becomes better defined. (You approach within 5 metres of this pole, and then your path heads straight down, soon parallel with the line of poles) The general direction of descent is clear enough, even if the precise path is not. Keep to the left towards the poles if in doubt.

A small reservoir with an aqueduct becomes visible below you, to your SE, and just above it your onward path is clearly visible.

Your path leads you down to *a little bridge over a mini-gorge.* The bridge has breeze block sides to it. It is now within about 20 minutes of your first sighting of Erquito.

You go over the bridge and to the right – you are now above the reservoir. Your path onwards is Southwards, heading below all the houses of Upper Erquito. You pass in front of a house to your left hand side with a green door and three windows (and several houses above it), continuing straight on, your direction Southwards/190 degrees. In 15 metres, ignore a well-defined path going down to your right, Westwards (with big stones on either side). In 20

55

metres, you pass under telephone cables and below under a hut with two green doors to your left hand side and onwards towards more houses. 100 metres from the hut, you *come up onto a car road and turn right along it,* Southwards. In 150 metres, you cross a streambed below you and continue onwards. In 20 metres, you pass a white house with two metal doors on your right hand side. *Opposite the end wall of the house, you need to take a faint path up and to your left, towards the houses above,* with a view to following the telegraph poles up through the village.

In 15 metres your path is paved and heads up ESE/110 degrees, going to the left hand side of the houses above. Once at the top, from the last house and the last telegraph pole in the village, carry on along the paved path, still steeply upwards and Southwards.

Within 10 minutes or so of becoming wider, this major trail becomes thinner again, but is still cobbled and easy to follow. Your way ahead is visible on the far hillside above a series of green terraces looking like narrow steps up a staircase. Your way continues across a small patch of rocks, heading SW initially; then quite steeply up to get out of the barranco.

Soon you can see a part of your path ahead that is supported from underneath by a high parapet or terrace of rocks. (Ignore a fork left here, going off Eastwards/85 degrees.) Within five minutes of this parapet, you can see the main tarmac road immensely far below you to your right (this road leads to La Dama). At this point, I feel on top of the world and that a stone dropped over the edge of the barranco would fall a kilometre before hitting the bottom, and I pitied the Spaniards attempting to conquer this impenetrable island.

Within 5 minutes of this parapet, you come to a 'Paisaje Protegido' National Park sign. I tend to eat my lunch near here.

Your way onwards is clear when you encounter a patch of grey rock – your path continues, initially SSE/160 degrees. Within about 30 minutes from the parapet-supported bit of path, and just before a drystone house to your left hand side with a collapsed roof, your trail broadens out into a track broad enough for a car, which you continue on (not the fainter track to your SW towards houses in the distance).

Within 12 minutes or so of your trail broadening out, on turning a bend you see El Drago (three or four house complexes, the first one with a fence round its garden) to the SW (with the village of Arguayoda beyond and nearer to the sea). *You come to a T-junction where the wide trail you are now on joins a loop of asphalted road. You don't take this road, but instead, 5 metres before this T-junction, you head on an ill-defined trail to the right* that will lead in due course to El Drago (the hamlet is SW/220 degrees from you) though you initially head WNW/290 degrees, *almost back on yourself.* In 10 metres you are 10 metres below an almond tree to your right hand side, on a path with a terrace of rocks also to your right hand side. *At the very far end of the terraces, almost to the edge of the barranco, your path at last turns left*, a wide path towards El Drago, your direction SSW/205 degrees. Keep towards **El Drago**, following a waterpipe in for the last 100 metres. The first house with the fence around it is the one that gave me water, murky water from a big flagon.

Continue on down through the hamlet, keeping to the left and following the waterpipe. Pass by the side of the richly-renovated house complex called Villa Silvesde, to your right hand side, and down its concrete steps and straight on down an asphalted road, either scrambling down the terrace to the 'main' car road, or veering left with this asphalted drive, in 50 metres to the car road, *where you turn right,* your direction WNW/290 degrees, (towards Arguayoda). You are now leaving the German map's route 16 and you will soon be taking a route to meet up with their route 57 into Alajero.

Passing empty houses you leave El Drago there is a steep bend leftwards at the last renovated white house complex with its palm trees.

Within 300 metres of leaving, you pass a drystone house with a collapsed roof on your right, your direction at this point being SE. In fine weather, you may be able to glimpse the outskirts of Alajero, still two barrancos away, ESE/110 degrees from you. *At the next sharp bend, where the main tarmac road you are on goes off WNW/290 degrees, you go left on an earth car track*, signposted La Manteca, initially in a SE/125 degrees direction, and soon passing a 'Passaje Protegido' sign.

The path is now heading down towards the edge of the barranco. Within 3 minutes or so of joining this track, you see the erstwhile deserted village of **La Manteca** below you. It looks down into a magnificent barranco. Two houses have now at last been renovated here (one by a German, the other by a Spaniard) and it is places like this that I would particularly like to see restored to full life. In my vision there would be houses for rent to aspiring artists and writers, and a pension with café and shop for walkers. I have even made contact with a solicitor of honest appearance who seems to share my views about alternative tourist development on Gomera, and would be prepared to research and to act for would-be purchasers of land in this area. His grandfather used to own much of the land at La Cantera on the coast near here. His name is Humberto Negrin Mora, c/o San Francisco No. 5, 7° Piso, Edificio Santander, Santa Cruz, Tenerife (tel 922 28 34 89, fax 922 28 80 51).

Keep to the main path down through La Manteca and resist two opportunities to go left towards ledges with huts built into the caves. A young German who had got tired walking was planning to stay overnight without a sleeping bag in the lower ledge hut when I was there, but I preferred to press on in the dusk. This was the barranco I ran down, but I have added to my sketchy first edition directions with details from re-doing this walk more slowly in subsequent years.

Head down, keeping to the right, past a big house with three green doors, and your track down into the barranco is to your right. Within 10 minutes, *you come to a T-junction*, above a goat's house built in the rocks. Ignore leftwards – NNW/335 degrees – although it offers a clear onward and terraced, horizontal path, and *take the main right fork ever downwards*. Below you, you can see a house complex out on a promontory of rock at the bottom of the barranco which you will be passing close to (if I were a millionaire, I would live here, with a cable car to take me up and down the barranco). Soon you can see a little green water reservoir below you. *At a T-junction*, just after seeing the reservoir for the first time, with main paths going both ways, *go left* (your way marked by a mini-cairn and your direction ENE/70 degrees) heading to cross the stream below. Soon you cross a streambed of pink rock and you go up the other side, a continuation that is straight on for 5 metres Eastwards then up and to your left. There is a white-painted horizontal aqueduct 30 metres above you, and a mini-cairn showing that you are on the correct path up. You cross over the disused aqueduct you saw from below. And there is a red stripe on the rock to your right for further reassurance.

Within a couple of minutes from the aqueduct, you pass on the right my three or so millionaire houses, mere ruins at present, out on the promontory (the one at the far end has a good roof and floor and has evidently been used by passers-by needing a night's kip) Then your way is past a ruined breeze-block house on your right, and within 5 minutes of this, you cross over more rocks marking the streambed. Your continuation is straight on and up, on a defined path, initially in an ESE/115 degrees direction. In 50 metres your path again crosses the streambed, with mini-pools here, and your onward path is up to the right, initially in a Westerly direction.

Going up the barranco is unproblematic – at one point, as you cross red rocks, the path is less well-defined, but heading in the direction ESE/120 degrees, you soon pick up the mini-cairns and upward path (ignore the faint fork to the right). Head to the left of the crag above you, and within three minutes, ignore the fork to the left (where you can touch the rock that overhangs your path) and continue more in the straight on direction (WNW/290 degrees) towards and up the carved steps in the rock. Very near the top, keep to the left, alongside a rock embankment (avoiding the just possible right hand path horizontally along the top of terraces). You have a fine view back across to La Manteca.

Virtually at the top, and marked by two mini-cairns like doorposts, and by red slash on the rock to your left, you turn left and follow a well-defined path, between terraces to the right of you and rocks to the left of you, initially in an Easterly direction.

You see a house 200 metres above you, slightly to the right. (This house, which used to be a ruin, has been leased for several years by Ernst from Germany, who has been very hospitable to us, giving us water and lemon grass tea. He lives there year-round, making sculptures and a vegetable garden, and in Feb 2001 was planning to acquire two goats, meanwhile having five cats and a dog. His spare room might suit a lodger who would like to live for a while in the middle of nowhere, in harmony with nature, without electricity or running water.)

Eventually this path turns upwards to the right, does the zig (of a zigzag) and continues in the same direction as before.

You immediately *pass the house to your right hand side and continue straight on. In 10 metres you cross over cream-coloured rocks, your direction half left, SE/130 degrees.* There are mini-caves away to your left (one with a man-made window). *You can soon see the asphalted car road ahead, go to it and turn left along it.* You can glimpse your final destination on the far hillside, Alajero, with a final easy barranco between you and it, and East/85 degrees from you.

(If you want to avoid the last barranco, keep on up this road to the main road, where you turn right for Alajero, trying for a lift. But the main walk directions continue:) You go down the gentle incline and then up. You see a white house on your right, fringed with palm trees. (This house was occupied by German sea biologists under the name 'Orca Adventures'.) *Just 10 metres beyond a new concrete water tunnel under the road, take the initially concreted path to the right towards the house, and turn left 5 m before its 'Privado' barrier, on a path between terrace walls,* your direction ENE/70 degrees – thus having the wall of the house's garden to your right hand side. In 25 metres, veer right with this path, your direction now SSE/155 degrees. In a further 100 metres, you follow a thin metal waterpipe alongside your way, for 300 metres, heading up towards a large desirable-looking two storey white house with outhouses. At which point, and with the house still a 100 metres away, and *by the first palm tree, your path heads down,* initially NE/40 degrees, down towards the noise of the frogs below on the barranco floor.

The path down is straightforward. You see a large reservoir below you. You cross the streambed and continue on. *30 metres before the reservoir, by a big isolated boulder marked 'A' with a mini-cairn on top of it, you go left,* your direction ESE/120 degrees, on a faint path round the left hand side of the reservoir, bearing right and upwards. Just above the reservoir, ignore a cobbled path going down to your right and continue upwards over rocks, your direction Eastwards. In 30 metres you have a defined path upwards.

I recorded this barranco for the first edition by moonlight, although it took me an hour of experimenting and waiting for the moon to climb. If I can do it by moonlight, I suspect you will find the route simple to find by daylight.

You zigzag your way to the top, keeping to the main path.

Once at the top, your continuation path is easy, a car-broad track initially South, that takes you into Alajero.

Alajero

Soon you will see the church to your right, and you can then

Alajeró

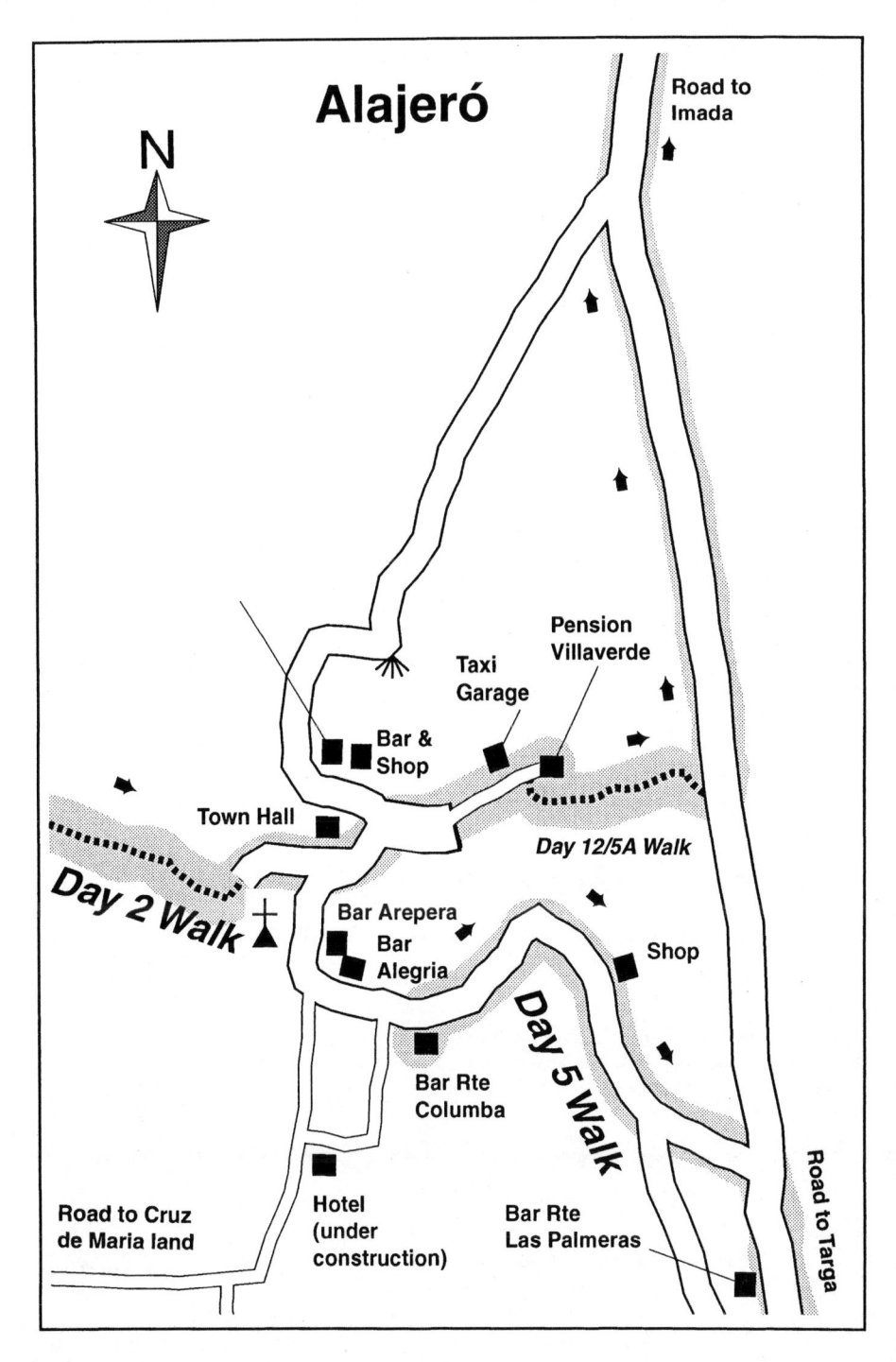

N

Road to Imada

Pension Villaverde

Taxi Garage

Bar & Shop

Town Hall

Day 12/5A Walk

Day 2 Walk

Bar Arepera

Bar Alegria

Shop

Day 5 Walk

Bar Rte Columba

Hotel (under construction)

Road to Cruz de Maria land

Bar Rte Las Palmeras

Road to Targa

turn off your path, down to the paved square behind the church. Go up past the left hand side of the church onto the asphalt road, and keep on it upwards to the ENE/ 70 degrees, past the taxi rank on your right. Keep straight on the same road, past the town hall on your left, and the low white terraced building on your right (Hilda Villaverde's always-closed shop, where she can sometimes be found if not at the pension). At the very end of the road, at the edge of the town, just beyond a magnificently huge eucalyptus tree on your left, is the very fine **Pension Villaverde** (tel 922 895162), run by the hospitable Hilda Villaverde, whose brother owns a big house the other side of the hill and whose nephews and nieces are at various universities or holding down high-powered jobs. She charges 4,000 pesetas for a room for two people for one night (longer periods may be at a lowerer rate) – if you are planning to follow my suggestion for Day 5 in this booklet, you will book with Hilda for a second night too at this point. The balcony rooms are preferable, if free. There are also two apartments with their own kitchens, which are the finest option, if available for short stays. If she is full and there are no alternatives, the **taxi** stored in the garage next to her pension and driven by her brother (tel 922 895140 or book through Hilda) could take you on to another town – it can seat six –

although it might be worth asking in the town's bars for alternatives or for someone willing to put you up.

Hilda's pension is more luxurious than most Gomeran ones, with at least a small amount of hot water in the showers, towels and a fine balcony overhung by the branches of a tree laden with delicious oranges.

In 2000 and 2001, a large hotel to the South of Alojero's sports field was still under construction. I have also seen advertised **Casas Don Pedro**, two renovated houses which are bookable by phoning a German number (tel 00 49 69 44 20 23).

There are two unmarked **shops** nearby, one (more a bar than a shop) just on the North side of the town hall, up some steps behind it – and for the other shop (which has a slightly wider range) you go down past the primary school and football pitch, with the **Alegria town bar** opposite (this bar will sell you peppers, rolls, cheese and fruit), and keeping left you pass the Bar Columba to your right hand side and go on for several hundred metres. There, the first house after the road curves right, is a small shop with a green door, again up some steps. Even on Sundays it is 'open' till 11pm. What this means is that if the light is on, you can ring the doorbell, even if the door is locked, and the shopkeeper lady will appear.

The **Bar Columba** has the best food, and is run by Antonio, a friendly and very

deaf old man, assisted by Callos his son and Helga, a German assistant who lives locally. Besides the town bar, there is also nowadays a hamburger bar.

Buses leave from the bus shelter in upper Alajero, on the main road between San Sebastian and Santiago. These line 3 buses go at (*= not Sunday or festival days) 5.45am*, 8.15am, 12.45pm*, 4pm, 5pm* for Santiago, then on to Tecina Hotel, Las Toscas, Degollada de Peraza and San Sebastian.

To visit the island's only **dragon tree**, see the detour at the start of Day 5 Alternative Alajero to Santiago walk, below.

Day 5: A round trip back to Alajero via Imada

Toughness: 6 (not for vertigo sufferers). Beauty: 9. Hours: 6.

Alajero is my favourite town on the island, and worth a second night. You may also feel it is time for a less strenuous day's walking. The Imada valley, at least the last part leading into Imada, is supremely beautiful. Santiago is a disappointingly ugly tourist town and worth avoiding, and the route onwards from Santiago to San Sebastian is majestic in only a rather barren way and is hard work (although it does offer a good enough beach for swimming). So, on balance (for the Santiago option has its attractions) an easy round trip back to Alajero is on my main menu for Day 5. Have a late start, take the climbing really slowly and you will still be back well before sundown. The route goes via the hamlet of Targa down steeply on route 45 to Guarimiar and then mostly uphill (less steeply) towards Imada (on the way there are abandoned houses to explore and fine spots under almond trees to have a snooze). In Imada you may find the one bar open, even on a Sunday, and, in the evening, the community centre bar too (there is no pension or place to stay). You could call for the Alajero taxi from Imada or take route 44 steeply uphill back to the main road or follow the more gentle tarmac road and/or goat tracks back out of Imada to this main road (then it is a matter of walking or hitching a lift back to Alajero).

For those wanting more activity: in the morning before setting out, you could visit the remains of the **Cruz de Maria** social experiment, two kilometres from Alajero, described earlier in this booklet under 'Social experiments'. (I would welcome a report as to whether there are renewed signs of activity on site.)

Or you could do the Day 5 Alternative walk and hitch or get a bus back from Santiago to Alajero afterwards. I confess that often this is our preferred walk if we are tired by day 5, since it is flat or downhill most of the day and I have been tempted to promote it to main walk status.

This Day 5 Alternative walk is also the one for purists wanting to complete the circuit of the island on foot. It consists of following tracks to Imada, then down route 42 to El Azadoe and Benchijigua (a village that is being developed as a centre for ecological experiments, complete with solar street lighting) and route 41 to Santiago, where you can stay the night. Apart from the last three kilometres or so walking beside a quarry, and the disappointments of arriving in Santiago, the remainder of this Day 5 Alternative walk is delightful. It takes between 6 and 7.5 hours and is a very easy 20km walk, with relatively easy route-finding.

For those on the main Day 5 walk from Alajero to Imada: *As if coming out of the Bar Columba in Alajero, turn right* and continue along the asphalt road. 500 metres past the bar, bend with the road sharply to the right, past the town's main shop (see above) and *take the first asphalt road fork up to the left, joining the main road and continuing on to the right.*

Soon you can see the new Santiago airport out by the sea (to your SE) behind a large dam wall.

Your turning to Targa when it comes is signposted and the road is asphalted. Targa is within metres of the turn-off (not the kilometre indicated on the German map). You go into **Targa**, a hamlet of a few houses, continuing round the bend to the right, *passing all the houses, and ignoring the asphalt road as it forks left at the bend*, continuing on the non-asphalt road track. Your trail down the barranco is a turn-off to the left – to find it you go past a smart house with two green windows plus occasional inlaid stones on the white wall, then *past a drystone shed, and in 50 metres you go over a small metal waterpipe to reach your trail going off to the left*, initially ENE, marked by a hand-painted sign in green paint with an arrow towards Santiago and Guillamar. (The trail is 10 metres before a huge quarry hole on the left of the road, in case you go too far along the road.)

Immediately you have an impressive view of the barranco that you will shortly be zigzagging down, with El Rumbazo visible below you. Your main trail down is not hard to follow; ignore any minor turn-offs. On the way down you come to a wide aqueduct on your left. Just after the aqueduct, says Christine Holloway, 'the path splits; take the right hand path, continuing downhill, not the path to the left which goes along the contour parallel to (but below) the aqueduct'. Later I have had in the past to push my way through overhanging dead palm branches.

Within 45 minutes of starting down the barranco, the bottom is reached, and the aim thereafter is to go left, following the streambed valley at varying distances below you to your right, and bearing in mind that your destination Imada will remain invisible for a long time to your NW.

In the meantime, *you come down to two houses and a ruined drystone hut. Your way is, as mentioned, to the left, initially NW, with a waterpipe above you* (on your left) for a few metres. (On this walk into Imada, you cross other walking routes, and so the mini-cairns and red dots are not wholly reliable indicators of your onward path.) Within half a minute you *carry on with the main path* to the left (a faint fork right goes towards a house with a broken tiled roof). Soon you cross back over the waterpipe and later over a fallen palm tree. And the path is upwards. When a faint path offers a way forward, carry on up to the left, initially NNW/340 degrees, on the main red rock path. (I have put a row of small stones to bar the way across the faint path.)

You can now see more clearly a small white chapel on the far hillside to your NNE/20 degrees, with a substantial white balustrade wall under it.

About 300 metres past the chapel, *you come to a main cobbled path going off sharp left (SSW 200 degrees) and then off steeply uphill. Ignore this.* The fainter path marked by a mini-cairn (and by a red dot on the right hand side 8 metres further on) is the more interesting one to take, going straight on (WNW/290 degrees initially).

(To pinpoint this turn further: There is a long house on the opposite side of the valley at this point, to your NNE/20 degrees, which is two derelict huts joined together, with another hut 30 metres above it and to the left.)

You continue past two drystone houses in reasonable condition but empty, with an adjoining oven under a huge rock. 30 metres past these houses, *you come to another fork, with straight-on looking as if it heads for two white houses with red doors up above you (WNW/290 degrees from you). But your path is sharply to the left and uphill,* your direction 135 degrees. Within 100 metres of going steeply uphill from this fork, *you come to a T-junction, under a palm tree, and you turn right,* initially WNW/290 degrees, a direction that is marked by a pink dot 6 metres ahead of you.

In a further 45 metres, you pass a drystone house with three walls and no front wall and no roof. In 50 metres beyond this, a substantial fork left uphill offers itself, heading SSE/160 degrees initially, whilst *the path straight on has in sight within 50 metres a drystone house – take this path, not the uphill one* (unless the suggested path has become very obstructed). You come to the drystone house has a tiled roof in good condition with beyond it an extraordinary animal shelter with a giant rock for a roof. The path continues past this house.

(Ignore a further fork to the left uphill.) Your path is initially NNE/20 degrees. Above, you glimpse to the left a house made of what looks like red breeze blocks with white mortar, and with a cliff overhang for a roof. You pass by under this, keeping to the main path. You are now more or less parallel to the streambed.

You pass ruins and abandoned houses on the right, and another breeze block house, more brown than red this time, on the left, and then more houses to the left and right, and a high fenced garden of orange and avocado and other trees (whose fence you can touch on your right hand side).

You pass two ruined houses on your left, and your path follows a water pipe.

Where the water pipe runs 8 foot above the ground to your right, 10 metres away from you, and where the trail forks, one way following the water pipe, and one to the left uphill, take the uphill fork, initially NW, and marked by a mini-cairn and red dots.

You will soon see violet paint graffiti on a boulder saying 'und jetzt ein Erdinger im Case Flora'.

Soon you are following the streambed valley again, and parallel to a waterpipe on the far side of the valley that follows the route of an old aqueduct.

Round a bend, you see to your left (WNW/290 degrees) black stains on the rock face, the remains left by a huge waterfall.

There is still no sign of

Imada, and the path is seemingly endlessly upwards and onwards, although the gradient is gentle enough.

You come alongside a wide old aqueduct and your path levels out. You cross a small waterpipe and immediately cross the aqueduct, following the waterpipe and the main path up (to your leftwards, initially NW).

You come to a spectacular steep drop down to your right. A little way further, if you peer bravely over the edge, you can see an aqueduct below you tunneling into the sheer cliff, a small miracle of engineering.

At last you can see Imada, to your WNW/290 degrees. There are several beautiful places between here and the village to lie out under the almond trees – many in full blossom in January.

The path is soon up rocks, with no clear definition, but the general direction is evident. You pass a ruined drystone house on your left.

You follow the main cobbled path up to your NW (not the faint path right). This fork is by a palm tree to the left of the fork.

There is a red circle 20 metres up from this fork and you join a waterpipe going in your direction. You cross the waterpipe, still going directly up in Imada's direction (ignoring a lower path parallel below yours). *Keep on the main boulder-paved path up, ignoring all other ways, and heading up towards the very left edge of town.*

About 80 metres from the topmost village buildings, a short-cut into **Imada** *is to fork right (after the turn right with the large waterpipe) towards a breeze-block shed* 30 metres ahead of you and to go on a narrow ledge over a mini-streambed, and up to the right below house terrace walls, going right and horizontal towards the electricity sub-station and then up to the left, up steps between houses, keeping on up these steps to the asphalt road.

Imada

Turning right on the asphalt road, you come in 100 metres to the new two storey community centre building which has a public bar in the back, open in the evenings from 6pm to 10 or 11pm (the house has a tiled roof, an arched doorway, and four tall but ultra thin windows to the right of the door). *400 metres further on, the road comes to an end,* and you come to a telephone box with behind it a mural of a bird flying towards the sun, and opposite, a bar at No.49, the **Bar Cafeteria Arcilia** (tel 922 895 395). This place, open daily (closed Friday) from 9.30am to 3pm and 5pm to 11pm, used to be run, before its modernisation, by a little old woman called Nieves Hernandes who was helpful beyond the call of duty – she is still around, but the place is now run by her daughter.

I am told you may be able to get a room in Imada for the night if you are lost.

In the meantime, *the on-ward route is from* (on the right hand side, facing the entrance) *straight uphill* on a new tarmac road (route 44 – if you cannot face this steep climb, go back to Alajero on the much gentler main road or the paths out of Imada – and still a beautiful walk). You go up this road for 50 metres, then turn left up a wide track, your direction WNW/310 degrees. On the uphill track, you pass on your left a little shed with near it an abandoned railway line and machinery leading into a mining tunnel.

You, however, continue uphill without deviation. An hour or so up from Imada you *come out through a posh cobbled entrance way to the main road. Turn left and get a lift or walk back to **Alajero**.*

Back on the outskirts of Alajero, *ignore a first sign saying Alajero Casco to your right.* You come to a rusty yellow VW displayed on a roof by the road side on your left. Then in 50 metres *there is a turn off to Alajero to your right. Don't take it. In about 600 metres, by the first palm tree on your right as you come downhill, turn sharp right onto a car track,* initially NW, and then immediately, *after 20 metres, left and down to the streambed and across towards the first substantial house* on the hillside opposite. This is the Pension Villaverde.

Day 5 Alternative A: Alajero to Santiago

Toughness: 5. Beauty: 8. Hours: 7.5.

There cannot be many towns in the world with such beautiful exit routes: *leaving Alajero's Pension Villaverde along the bottom of the house and to the left*, you pass above rocks pools and past almond trees. At a fork after 50 metres, ignore the left fork with a white arrow on the rock, and go right, then slightly to the left across a streambed and up a path between rocks. Go left at a T-junction and then right up to the road. Turn left on this road. (If you are ever hitching back to the pension, and want to be dropped off here, note that this path leads off the road by the last palm tree lining the road going upwards.)

(If you would like to take a steep detour to the island's only **dragon tree**, adding 40 minutes or so to your journey time, take a fork to the left off the main road just beyond the Alajero Casco road sign and immediately by the bus stop. You walk between terraces, soon passing a new (industrial?) building under construction to your right hand side, your direction is due North. You carry on between terraces till you come to a junction where up leads to a mirador or 'viewing platform' – this is your exit route for later. For now you go down to a tarmac road, with a signed footpath off to the dragon tree. Just before a lower mirador, go left and down. Then after admiring the tree, it's up to the top mirador and the main road, then follow the road signs to Imada.)

Assuming you are not detouring to the dragon tree, you can either *hitch to Imada*, which is signposted down and off the main road to your right, about 3 or 4 kilometres after leaving Alojero; or *walk to Imada mainly on paths*. For the latter very pleasant option, leave Alajero on the tarmac road uphill in the direction of Imada. Once past the bus shelter, the road goes past the (industrial?) building under construction, mentioned above, with this building to your left hand side, and bends in a curve to the right. Below a little complex of houses above you to your right hand side, *fork right off the tarmac road onto the very clear donkey path that sets off upwards* due North towards Imada. In 40 metres cross the drive that leads to the houses and continue on upwards towards a pylon. This path rejoins the tarmac as it crosses the highest point between Alajero and Imada. Go right on the tarmac for about 75 metres, to a gap in the car balustrade, and follow *concrete steps on the right down to a path to Imada*.. Cross over the next tarmac you come to and continue down the other side, slightly to your right. At the next road crossing, go left and in 250 metres, 30 metres beyond a pylon, take the path down, initially NNW/330 degrees, towards the village. At the next encounter with tarmac, on the edge of **Imada**, go right downhill for 50 metres, then turn left by the lamppost onto a path, your direction NW/320 degrees. Follow the lampposts and path *to an electricity substation* below the village, at which point you *turn left up steps* to the castellated road above. Turn right on the road. In 100 metres you pass the community centre on your right hand side.

Go right *through the village on the main road until it comes to an end*. There is the **Bar Cafeteria Arcilia** on your left (described above, see Day 5). *Go leftwards along your side of the building with the mural on it*, towards El Azadoe (if you are asking directions, it's pronounced 'El Azadoi') – the path goes roughly Eastwards. *At the first bend*, with house No. 66 ahead of you (the house number is visible in the basement, under some concrete steps) and with one waterpipe going down and another going left, *take the left turn, and follow the trail down to your right (not the immediate concreted way up to your left)* – the first few steps at this fork are in a Northerly direction. A few metres down this path you join two large waterpipes heading down. Your direction is now SE.

Heading downwards the waterpipe that remains with you is a thin one on your right and you are between terraces on both sides.

Cross a big waterpipe and

ignore a turn right uphill. In 15 metres, ignore a faint way ahead. Stay on the main path.

You cross a big waterpipe and come to a red rock streambed.

You go over another large waterpipe the other side and up a well-defined path marked by a line of rocks to your right, your direction SE/145 degrees.

Within 30 metres you pick up a small thin metal waterpipe on your left, and ignore, 20 metres on, a turn-off path to the left (going steeply up).

At the telegraph pole, your main way veers left up carved red rock steps, well above and to the right of a house with two hut outhouse. Before passing the house, you will find that the thin waterpipe on your right is joined by one on your left.

At the top of the first flight of steps, your path leads on with more steps to a second house (with a telephone pole attached and a detached outhouse).

You are now parallel to the main car road out of Imada (on the opposite side of the valley).

Just past this house you may have a grand view down the Imada valley all the way to Santiago. Your general aim is to head over a high ridge into the next main valley.

The path is more or less level as it curves around the valley. Ignore any faint turn-offs.

You lose sight of most of Imada within 20 minutes of leaving the village.

Ignore a faint fork downwards and keep to the main path and then ignore a fork off up the hill.

At a corner, about 15 minutes from the previous houses, you have a view of a somewhat ruined house complex just 30 metres below you.

Just round the corner and still before coming down to the house complex, *you come to a T-junction,* ignore the left way, due North, and *take the right hand way towards the houses,* initially SSE/160 degrees, the path that evidently connects with your onward path on the other side of the valley.

You now pass (20 metres away to your right hand side) the fallen-down drystone wall of the outer building of the house complex, and you continue on down, your direction 15 degrees, keeping to the main path – down over a streambed.

Then the path is up towards a rock on the skyline ahead with a nipple on its top, and with the hamlet of **El Azadoe** and its nine houses beneath it. *About 500 metres from the hamlet, which is now to your SE, ignore paths equally well-defined going off uphill* (initially Eastwards) and keep down towards the hamlet.

Keep to the main path. At the ridge, if you go up to the rock shaped by nature somewhat in the form of a mushroom (and which has Coto de Caza painted in big white letters on it) you will see below you, to your ENE/60 degrees, the village of Lo del Gato, and Imada to the West/280 degrees behind you, and the pear-shaped Rock Agando to the ENE/75 degrees, with Benchijigua, your interim destination, a kilometre below Rock Agando.

35 metres from the mushroom rock, in your previous direction, you bear left *over the ridge* out of your present valley. DO NOT take the right hand fork (which looks almost straight on). So you go to the left of the crag with the nipple and then down to the right. Soon ignore the minor fork to the right (which goes along the left of the ridge to El Cabezo) and take the left fork going lower down.

Keep to the main trail down, with a red dot on your left. You come to an abandoned white house, with two doors and no windows, and a kiln-shaped drystone bread oven to the right and two ruined outhouses on the left. (If you look inside, you will see that the roof is made up of bamboo, then polythene, then interlocking tiles. Within ten years, I am sure that this house too will be an expensive winter home and office for some international business person.)

Travelling on, initially NNW/335 degrees, you cross a streambed and ignore the faint path down it to the right, to carry on, your direction ENE/70 degrees. Within a couple of minutes, you see houses below you (Lo del Gato).

Carry on the path for quite some time, until it ends

by coming down onto a wide car track. You turn left uphill on this, your direction NNW/340 degrees – there are a couple of tiled houses away to your right hand side. In due course, you cross a streambed (a big black electricity cable hanging across the streambed to your left hand side) and continue up into **Benchijigua**.

Benchijigua has apparently been funded as something of a showcase alternative energy project. It is recognisable from a distance by its solar street lighting. Two windmills are said to be planned. The Hotel Tecina has renovated several houses in the village.

Carry on up into the village. The first house you come to on your left hand side at the top, is the bar (tel 922 895404, or home number 895510) open daily from 10am to between 6pm and 8pm, depending on the amount of custom. (The road to the right at this point leads to the chapel with a rather interesting set of caves above it.). *Continuing on the main road, in 40 metres you pass a substantial breeze-block house on your left hand side, with three large windows, and then 5 metres past it, you leave the car track to go down to the right on a trail marked at its outset by a blue arrow and green dot,* in a direction that is initially NE/40 degrees. This leads down into a lovely grove of eucalyptus trees where we picnicked and watched the builders at work on a house, now finished – the first substantial renovation work I had seen in any non-mainstream village on the island. These houses are available for rental from the Fred Olsen Hotel Tecina company (tel 922 145864; from 7000 pesetas a day for two people. The caretaker for the houses is the woman who works in the Benchijigua bar.).

Keep on down the main trail between terraces past rocks on the streambed to your right hand side. Ignore a path off to the right that heads SSW/200 degrees. *You keep on the main path that goes along the bottom of the terraces* and below the already-mentioned renovated house complex. This is the spot overlooking the meadows where we picnicked.

Now you go over another streambed, and head predominantly Southwards. Your general aim is to follow the left side of the valley bottom all the way to Santiago. But in more detail: In 30 metres, ignore a faint fork left. In a further 70 metres, ignore a sharp left fork (heading initially NE). Continue towards the large tiled roof of a dilapidated house under a brow of rock. 30 metres before this house, take the main path away from it in an ENE/80 degrees direction, then 10 metres later *there is a small short-cut if you want it: you go right down a path*, past a palm tree (5 metres in) down beside the above-mentioned dilapidated house away to your right. Keep on the tarmac road, always in a downward Southwards direction, within 5 minutes *heading down to the bridge over the streambed. Turn left onto this car road, go over the bridge and continue on this car track South.*

100 metres uphill, you cross a tiny streambed – a trail joins yours from the left, which you would have been on if you had not taken the short cut. In a further 100 metres, Southwards along this car track, *5 metres before it bends left, below a minicrag, you go down a trail to the right, Southwards, down a stepped path*, marked with two fading yellow stripes and a mini-cairn.

Lo del Gata will be soon visible below you and the reservoir wall to your West. You are parallel to the road from Lo del Gato on the other side of the valley.

You go over a working aqueduct. *Keep always on the main path with a general tendency Southwards.* Within 10 minutes you pass a pylon 2 metres to your right hand side. Within 6 minutes, ignore a path down to the right Northwards towards Lo del Gato, and carry on Southwards. You pass a pylon 5 metres to the right of your path, and later, another pylon, again 5 metres to the right of your path. Within 5 minutes, you pass a pylon 2 metres to the left of the path.

You are now within 2 hours of leaving Benchijigua.

Within 4 minutes you pass two circular concrete reservoirs on your right and come to shallow pools of rather green grungy water, where a local peasant was amused to surprise me skinny dipping or, rather, trying to drip dry behind a rock wearing only my Chinese sombrero.

Your path is onwards along this streambed, Southwards, past, above on your right, a disused watermill below an old drystone brick building (the rush of water from above into the mill announces its presence).

30 metres past the mill, ignore a well made cobbled path that zigzags up and up WSW/260 degrees. Your route onwards is to follow the streambed on its left hand side. Watch out for the cobbled continuation of your path on the other side of the streambed, heading upwards due South. (It is 10 metres past the point on the other, West, side of the streambed where the large waterpipe goes from being white to rusty black).

Soon on your right hand side there is a very well-farmed valley, with orange trees, almond trees, fig trees and palms with dates and papayas.

You enter **Pastrana**. *Going up steps you are now on an asphalted road, all the way into Santiago*, still Southwards. There are tables to sit at and a coke machine on your right in a few hundred metres. Later, you pass a quarry on your right hand side which fascinated me. It seems to be running out of the kind of stones it crushes, the ones from the streambed. What will it do about this?

Santiago

Continuing on into Santiago, you cross a major road (which leads to a tunnel on your right hand side) and continue on, Southwards, down a minor road. You pass **Apartment Negrin** on your left hand side (tel and fax 922 895282, 2,500 pesetas for two). At the first T-junction, you see opposite you a grocery shop marked Tecina with a German 'Gemischt waren' sign. If you turn left here and go up past the third supermarket on the left hand side of the road (called Supermercada Laguna) and there turn left and up into Calle de Santa Rosa, you will find at the far end of the street on the left hand side at No. 56 (and already just visible from the supermarket) the **Casa Lolita**, where Senora Lola will rent you an entirely adequate room for 2000 pesetas for two people for one night, complete with a roof terrace with a fine view towards Santiago beach (tel 922 895234).

Other possible places to stay include:
Casa Huespedes Pension Nuestra Senora del Carmen, Avenida Maritima 18 (8 beds, tel 922 895028). This had little rooms for 2,500 pesetas for one night for two people, and was run by a very ancient lady.

Apartamentos Bella Vista, Calle Santa Ana (tel Enzo Musto 922 895208). 5,000 pesetas for two.

Apartamentos Casanova (above bar of the same name), Avenida Maritima (6 beds, tel 922 895002).

Apartamentos Mari Carmen, by the Calle de Santa Ana, off Paseo de la Laguna, (tel 922 895249 or 895271).

Pension La Gaviota (20 beds, tel 922 895135), Playa de Santiago, near the Alajero turn-off. 4,000 pesetas for two people for one night.

Luxury longer-term apartments up by the Tecina: **Apartamentos Santa Ana** (tel 922 895166).

There is a **bus** from Playa de Santiago leaving at (*= not Sunday or festival days) 11.45am, 3.15pm*, 6.45pm and 10.45pm* to Alajero; and to San Sebastian at 6.05am*, 8.35am, 1.05pm*, 4.20pm and 5.20pm* via the Tecina hotel, Las Toscas and Degollada de Peraza. A phone number for **taxis** in Santiago is 895022. A taxi back to Alajero cost us 1,500 pesetas in 2001.

The **tourist office** (offina de turismo) is at Ed. Las Vistas. Local 8, Avda. Maritima, s/n. Playa de Santiago (tel 922 865650).

If you end up with a day to spare in Santiago, the **motor yacht Siron** charges 6,000 pesetas to take you round the island (Sundays, Tuesdays and Thursdays, from 9am to 4pm).

Luxury hotel sauna

The sauna at the **Jardin Tecina** luxury hotel is open to non-residents, although those who answer the phone may not be aware of this and you may need to insist (1,000 pesetas for one hour, seem-

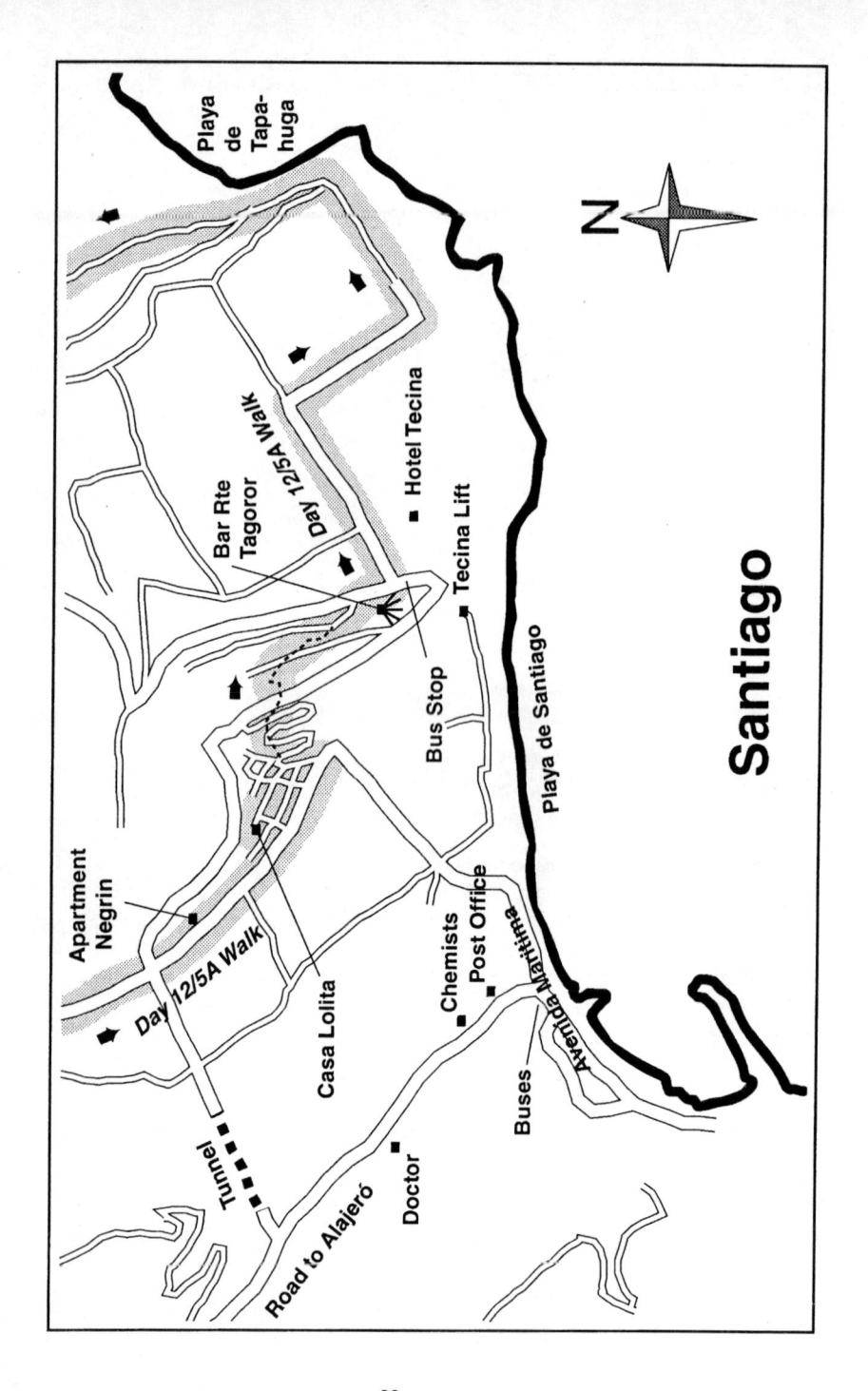
Playa de Tapa-huga
N
Day 12/5A Walk
Hotel Tecina
Bar Rte Tagoror
Tecina Lift
Bus Stop
Playa de Santiago
Santiago
Apartment Negrin
Day 12/5A Walk
Casa Lolita
Chemists
Post Office
Avenida Maritima
Buses
Tunnel
Road to Alajeró
Doctor

ingly irrespective of numbers; it is best to reserve your slot well in advance on 922 145864; it is closed on Sundays). On several visits, we have found this a pleasant refuge, which we had all to ourselves. You can lock the outer door, even washing and drying your clothes. One year towels were supplied, but at other times we have had to borrow some from the nearby toilets.

The most effortless way to get to the hotel, is to go to the seafront and turn left along it. You pass the Tecina's private bar and swimming pool on your left hand side and come to their lift (behind wooden doors). It's like something out of James Bond. At the top, you go up steps and then keep straight on, bearing left, till you reach the outdoor swimming pool. Go inside the main building and up to the first floor reception, where they will give you the sauna keys and point you in the right direction.

Afterwards, if you go out the front entrance (the other side to where you came in), going to the left brings you to the **Tagoror** restaurant. You can get a **bus** by turning right when coming out of the Tagoror – the stop is 30 metres to the right, on the other side of the road. The times for the buses, heading for San Sebastian via Santiago beach, are as above under Santiago La Playa, only 3 minutes earlier.

The hippie beach caves/yacht marina near Santiago

Toughness: 1. Beauty: 2. Hours: 1.

In 1996, my companion Bob persuaded me, against my better judgement, that despite having no sleeping bag, no sweater, no long johns and no mattress, we should try the foolish experiment of sleeping in one of the hippie beach caves near Santiago. The area where they are is zoned for a new yacht marina. Meanwhile, the way to these caves is also the way to start the Day 6 Alternative walk from Santiago to San Sebastian, and is as follows:

You go upwards along the asphalt road past Supermercado Laguna, the shop mentioned above, and follow it round. *70 metres from the supermarket, on the first bend, take the first of a series of steps that are short-cuts leading off the main road (another set of steps starts up by the church; at a fork in the steps go right).* At the top, turn right and this soon brings you to the Bar Restaurant **Tagoror** (at Tecina 93, tel 922 895425), on your right hand side. A previous year, this restaurant phoned up a cheap apartment for three of us in upper Santiago for one night. The restaurant has fine views from its dentist's chair down over Santiago, and serves delicious fish soup and sangria. Coming out of the restaurant, you turn right, and immediately left, *following a road sign to the Playa En Medio, passing in front of the huge Jardin Tecina complex, and then to the right, down the side of this complex, until you come nearly to the sea but also to the end of the banana plantation, at which point you turn left.*

You walk along past the Fred Olson agricultural building on your right hand side, to the first bay, which contains three large yellow building amongst other buildings down below. 300 metres along this bay, *at a road junction at the back of the bay, take the onward path, quarter right, up steps,* marked with a red dot, your direction initially 5 degrees. In 25 metres, you cross a track, to continue uphill over a large pipe. Cross the coast road, and continue on up a well-made path between terraces, marked with a red dot and a mini-cairn. By a telegraph pole at the top, cross an old aqueduct, and continue downwards the other side, rejoining the coast road by a sentry-size box. *Go left on the road.*

You are now overlooking the second beach, Playa de Tapahuga. Walkers to San Sebastian should take note of their onward path zig-zagging up the hill opposite. This beach is wide and has no buildings, although there were a couple of campers there. You walk round this bay; at the back, ignore a red dot path. At the end of the curve (and some 45 minutes after leaving Bar Restaurant

Tagoror) *you come to a fork, where the left hand fork says 'Private Property, Entry Forbidden'* and sometimes has a chain across the road. *This is the onward path for the walk to San Sebastian,* initially SE.

If, however, you want to visit the beach caves (and they do offer, at least at low tide, a short-cut way of rejoining the walk, without coming back to this fork) you take the right hand fork down to the beach, initially Southwards, and turn left along it, to the next beach, the Playa del Medio, where there used to be some cave-dwellers (no doubt now moved on) and where we stayed. Or carry on through a large hole in the rock, which is open at low tide, though neck high at high tide, to the next beach, Playa de Chinguarime, where there are more and slightly cleaner caves. (From this beach you can join the walk to San Sebastian by going up the banana plantations at the back of the beach and turning right by the fence described in the full walk details, below.) There are reputedly still more caves on the beach beyond this one. All these caves were raided by the police at 7pm a week before our visit, and another time they came at 10am. On the Playa de Chinguarime, they gave people time to take their belongings and then incinerated a token quantity of beach mats and whatever remained. There were no fines, and the cave dwellers were back within 48 hours. One German woman I spoke to rather resented the Hotel Tecina guests coming along the beach in the day time to gape at the cave-dwellers' every naked move. About 50 people live in the caves in the good times – carrying on a fine old Guanche tradition of cave-dwelling – but only a dozen or so were there on our night. I was shocked by the condition of our cave, it was so stereotypically hippy, as if German hippies feel some obligation to go the whole hog in the extreme opposite direction from mainstream society. There was broken glass under the sleeping area, congealed food and rubbish everywhere, and tea bags thrown up to stick on the cave ceiling for 'decor', with their strings and paper flaps moving in the wind. However tough the authorities decide to be on the cave people, they should at least recognise the realities of the situation and provide rubbish facilities. I also discovered that a space blanket is not large enough to wrap round my body to keep me warm, and that it gets quite cold at night even in fine weather in March at sea level.

Day 6: From Pajarito through the Parque National to El Cedro and Hermigua

Toughness: 7. Beauty: 6. Hours: 7.

This is probably the last day's walking, for those on a one week flight from London. In summary, Day 6 involves a walk, lift or taxi North from Alajero to the start of the walk 1.3 kilometres up from Pajarito. The Alajero taxi cost us 2,500 pesetas for 6 people in '98. The route is No. 28 on the German map, off right from the road (below La Laguna Grande on the map). It is a broad, flattish and to my taste over-popular and over-safe guarded official park trail (it has well-dug steps, neat bridges, numbered stages and even a handrail at times). There will be other walkers – some years these have been the first we have met on the same route as us for the whole week. The route passes beside a pleasant stream but has no views out of the forest, unlike the walk from Banda de las Rosas on Day 3. As far as El Cedro, it is more of a stroll than a walk. Those who want to miss the second much tougher part of the day could use the German map's route 27 into Hermigua. (This route from El Cedro to Hermigua is in fact very easy to follow – and is less arduous, but less delightful, than the main suggested route described below. This easier route has a lot of minor tarmac road at the end. Start at the La Vista restaurant balcony in El Cedro – which the main route below brings you to – and head down past their showers. Turn left where it's signposted to Hermigua. Ignore a fork right down to the waterfall. Go on down and down, and then eventually along the left hand edge of a small reservoir, across the reservoir barrier, and down the other side. Ignore a path up steps with bannisters, to the right of the reservoir. Soon there is a wide pipe along the path to your right hand side. You go down past a second reservoir. At a fork, follow the blue arrows down to the right. Soon you go left across a bridge with green railings and right on a minor tarmac road; then left down wide concrete steps towards a road bridge below. You go down to a tarmac road and turn left. Cross a bridge. You are in the outskirts of Hermigua.)

Another way of easing the day would be to take the car road from El Cedro up to the main road (see the asterisk below) and to catch a lift; or you could take the shortcut to this main road by going through the 600 metre tunnel (see the double asterisk below) from El Cedro (marked on the map as Wasserstollen 'El Rejo' and not recommended when there could be floods; this is a water channel and you might need a torch).

The whole day is primarily downhill. It is a fairly steep uphill climb out of El Cedro. Beyond El Cedro, you take an interesting and less used trail (mostly route 28) looping off to the North West to near Acevinos and then back to Hermigua via overgrown trails downhill to the Ermita de San Juan. For those who have one week only in Gomera, the idea is either to catch an evening bus or a taxi (which cost us 3,000 pesetas for 6 people in '98) from Hermigua to San Sebastian or to spend the night in Hermigua and then to catch a morning bus to San Sebastian – using San Sebastian as your base for last-minute shopping or walking.

If you should happen to be coming up for this walk from San Sebastian, you can catch either the Valle Gran Rey Line 1 bus leaving San Sebastian at 10.30am daily, arriving at Pajarito at 11.05am (check times locally).

Here is the full walk in more detail: From immediately in front of the pension in **Alajero**, take the beautiful footpath to the North West out of town. (See Day 5 Alternative, Imada to Santiago, for details.) *Once on the asphalt road, get a lift North on the road towards San Sebastian. Over four kilometres past the Imada turn-off is the turning left towards Chipude, but you go right and come to the **Pajarito** turn-off 1.5 kilometres further on.* Pajarito is simply a crossroads. *You take the road signposted Laguna Grande* (WNW/290 degrees initially). Within 8 minutes, you pass a road fork to your left (signposted 'Alto de Garajonay 1.4') and, on most occasions, a lot of parked cars. On your right hand side is the start of your walk, the **Alto de Contadero** at 1,350 metres, with a sign towards 'Arroyo de El Cedro 2.8' and 'Caserio de El Cedro 4.8'. The top layer of forest you will be passing through contains tree heathers, with a sharp transition from heather to larch (within 9 minutes of the start).

The path is made up with handrails and steps with wooden edges, but beware of these worn wooden edges, they are extremely slippery in the wet. Keep to the main path (eg within 3 minutes of setting out, fork left). Through the forest the main route keeps to paths near the streambed – several times there are choices of paths which later come together again.

Within an hour of starting this path, you come to post No. 11, and, to your right, a look-out point over the stream.

At post No. 13, follow the main route to the right (not the faint track straight on). In 20 metres, follow the right hand fork signposted 'Arroyo de El Cedro', your direction ENE/75 degrees. You come to post No. 15 and a 2 metre waterfall, with stone terraces supporting its top edges. There is a path along the top of the waterfall, but *your path is to ford over the lower rocks and to take the path off to the left*, initially NE, which goes up and parallel to the stream (to the right of it).

Soon you are following the stream as it forks right. You cross a simple wooden bridge, just wooden planks sideways, with a natural 'cave' 40 metres to your right formed by erosion of soil from under tree roots.

At post No. 16, your path

crosses a much wider, car-track-size road, about 40 metres from the bridge, and you turn down this to the right, heading NNE/20 degrees initially. Very soon, you *go over the river on the car track, through the car park and take the first fork left, the **Sendrero Forestal a la Ermita**, signposted 'Caserio de El Cedro 2.1'*. You go down bannisters and over a bridge also with bannisters.

Within 8 minutes, you come to another side-railed bridge, and then you go up on the left to the **Ermita N.S. de Lourdes** and to the ever-running drinking water in the picnic area.

As if coming out from the front door of the Ermita, you'll see to your front two trails off to the left, a lower and an upper one. Take the lower one (initially NNE/20 degrees), signposted 'Caserio de El Cedro 1.7', and keep to the main path (thus at the hint of a fork within 5 minutes, take the upper right hand fork, your direction ESE/ 105 degrees).

The many black olives on the ground are in fact sweet-smelling laurel berries, a potential business opportunity for the Body Shop if they are not already onto it.

Within 10 minutes of the Ermita you come to your first view into the rather picturesque El Cedro valley, and *a wooden sign on your right announcing 'Limite del Parque'*.

Take the right fork upwards here, not the left one which goes down earth steps. Your direction is initially Eastwards, towards a tiled long house.

You pass between various houses, with the El Cedro valley below you on your left. El Cedro is one of the few villages of the island which is already being substantially renovated. You come to the prohibitively priced £128,000 two storey house for sale with its 6,000 sq metres of land (for sale from Ocean Properties, tel 791262). Whilst we were there one year, a policeman was negotiating with Spanish squatters in the then empty building just above.

At a road junction, *go sharp left down, signposted to Bar Restaurante La Vista*. (If you carry straight on, the first house you come to is the old cafe, **Casa Prudencio**, which was closed in 2000 and 2001, but used to offer local food such as gofio with mojo, cheese, local wine and a sweet herbal liqueur made by the old man on the porch. The mainly earth road up from this house [*] leads within 3 kilometres to the main road, where you can get a lift either to Hermigua to your left or San Sebastian to your right.)

At the bottom of the hill in 60 metres is the entrance to the 600 metre **'El Rejo' water channel tunnel**, about 1.5 metres wide, heading SE, a short-cut to the highway for those wishing to drop out of the walk [**]. (My friend Sara went through this tunnel and says: "I had no torch and the candle the bar lent me shed insufficient light, so I just walked along in the dark. I'd taken my boots off as the water was ankle deep. It was smooth underfoot apart from having to creep over pebbles for the last few metres. At the end of the tunnel it's a very short distance to the road. It probably wouldn't be sensible to go this way when there are flash floods.")

Those continuing the walk should keep along the road towards the **La Vista restaurant** (tel 922 880944). The restaurant serves large meals at healthy prices It runs a camping site costing 300 pesetas per night per person and has information on local housing for rent. It also is the place to start from if you want the easier route to Hermigua described above in the introduction to this day.) At the T-junction before reaching the restaurant, with the restaurant 50 metres to your right, your onward path is left all the way up to the dead end (there may be a chain across marked 'Privado') then sharp right along the path on top of the terraces, your direction ENE/65 degrees (about 20 metres below a house with a short telephone pole growing out of its roof).

Stay on the main path (rather than forking left into this house's 'entrance' path).

Keep on the main trail at the next bend and go up concrete the concreted path. Soon ignore two fainter trail down off to the left. Carry on your path (now NNW/ 340 degrees). Soon you cross the earth drive of the **El Refugio** house to take the path up to the left, your direction NNW/330 degrees. In 20 metres you go up red earth steps, with the red-tiled roof of a new house to your right hand side.

It becomes mostly steep for quite some time, and the trees become bearded with moss again and you may be in cloud.

Near the very top, you go up some more stone steps and *at the top of these ignore a fork upwards and to the left marked with two green dots, leading initially NW/315 degrees*. Keep on the main trail, now at last downwards (initially NNW/340 degrees).

Within 4 minutes of this green dot turn-off, *you come to a car track and you turn right along it*, your direction NE/35 degrees. A large waterpipe immediately comes in on your left.

In a while you pass a street lamp with a house complex beneath it. This was for sale in 2001 (tel Eurocasa 922 872079) and as usual in such idyllic situations in Gomera, I wanted to be rich enough to buy it. Keep to the main path, ignoring ways off.

In due course, you pass a reservoir with outhouse on the left hand side of the track.

Soon after this, on a bend in the road, you ignore a path off to the left, marked with a mini-cairn and arrow. Within 3 minutes, *you come to a T-junction* – ignore the car track leftwards heading West, *you turn right along it*, Eastwards towards the sea.

In 30 metres or so, after the fork, and at the bend, you turn left down a footpath, marked with a cairn and a sign to say 'Senderos Alevinos San Juan', down steps, your direction ENE/75 degrees.

This way used to be very overgrown but has been now upgraded, too much so in my opinion, with safety railings and concrete. Your path is downwards, soon with a short bit of its continuation clearly visible on the hillside ahead to your ENE/70 degrees. *Within 8 minutes you join a car track, turning left along it, initially ENE/60 degrees*.

In 100 metres, *you come to a large distinctive (head-shaped?) rock on the path ahead of you, red in its lower half. At this rock, you keep on your main track as it bends back sharply on itself to the right*, now heading initially SW/215 degrees.

Follow this car-wide track, which threatens to become overgrown again very shortly, to a crazy paving look-out towards Hermigua below, with the Ermita de San Juan, your interim destination, below you to the ENE/70 degrees, on top of its own hillock.

If you peer right over the edge, you can see your continuation path below you, on the next hillside (direction ENE/65 degrees), as it curves round the valley towards the Ermita.

Carry on down the main path, ignoring any faint turn-offs. You come to your first stand of bamboo for the day,

on your right.

And within 4 minutes of that there is a look-out place with views to all sides and green metal railings. You can again see your Ermita continuation path (in an Easterly direction from you) three terraces below a hut with a corrugated roof.

Carry on down steps to your left, initially Westwards and away from your goal.

Within 3 minutes you come to a little mirador surrounded with green railings.

Within 2 minutes of this, you pass a house on your left, with its tiled roof beginning to fall in (and protected behind a high terrace wall).

Within 10 minutes of this house, you pass more metal railings to your right hand side and ignore a fork to your right which curves around the valley. You head away from the Ermita, going on the main trail, your direction NE/45 degrees..

Within 2 minutes, the path curves right and heads onto the path you could see from above, round the valley. At the next fork, in 1 minute, do not continue round the valley curve (SW/215 degrees) but instead follow the main path downwards (NE/50 degrees).

You pass a high drystone roofless square animal pen to the right hand side of the path. You go down past a drystone house (on your left) so ruined that it has almost surrendered to the vegetation. You go over a miniature streambed with an aqueduct on your right hand side. Now you are on a grassier path curving around the valley. (You may have to cross a corrugated iron barrier.)

Then there is a reservoir on your right. Carry on down towards the **Ermita de San Juan** and 100 metres before it, and now below it, *beside the end of the tarmac road coming up from below, follow the cobbled path forking off downwards (the end of the road to your right hand side)* your direction SE/145 degrees.

Carry on over the main apshalt road you come to (going very slightly to the left in doing so) and continue on down, on more steps.

After these, you go down an asphalt road to your left for a bit, and 15 metres after its first bend, you fork off left down a concreted cobbled path, initially NW, which you can see continuing on below you. Keep on the main path down.

There are no more shortcuts after this. *You come to the main road into Hermigua, and turn left along it,* passing the **Hotel Villa de Hermigua** on your left hand side, and then with a friendly bar, **Don Juan**, very shortly on your left.

Buses from near the main church in Hermigua go to San Sebastian (see Hermigua earlier in the book for more details). The **taxi** rank is here too.

You may want to continue on to lower Hermigua, perhaps stopping for a meal at the Casa Creativa on the way.

Day 6 Alternative: Santiago to San Sebastian

Toughness: 8. Beauty: 5. Hours: 9.

Those who reach Santiago on the Day 5 Alternative could then complete their circuit of the island on foot, with no transport involved, by following the coastal route (through rather bare countryside) from Santiago to San Sebastian. This 19 kilometre walk could take up to about 9 hours, with hard route finding for the first part, although it is all extremely easy from El Cabrito onwards. On the map it is route 40, then route 55 to **Casas de Contrera** (abandoned); then further inland to **Seima** (abandoned) followed by route 39 to **El Cabrito** community which has its own beach. This interesting Austrian community is described under 'Social Experiments' in this guide. They were very kind to us in 1999 when we arrived there wet and cold during a storm – drying our clothes for us and selling us a lovely hot meal. They run a **boat** that may be able to give you a 1,000 pesetas lift to San Sebastian which would save you from the last hour and a half or two hours of easy route finding and fairly gentle walking (Mareke or Hans Hubricht in El Cabrito both speak English, and could give you guidance about your onward path, if needed. Their boat to San Sebastian leaves at 4.40pm and 6pm in the afternoons – Sundays only 6pm. It is best to book a place in advance, tel 922 871233. Priority places are for their workers and guests). If you miss this boat there is no other way of shortening this walk, short of paying them 5,000 pesetas to arrange a special boat trip for you. So normally you should leave enough time to continue on by route 38 to San Sebastian. You can swim from the beach at El Cabrito, or from the nicer beach at **Playa de la Guancha**, in the next bay beyond it.

On my second attempt to find the right way, we got hopelessly lost on this route – we did not go far enough inland at the beginning and missed Casas de Contrera and Seima altogether. But we had an adventurous time 'off piste', going below the line of the pylons, parallel to them, finding ways up and down four or five barrancos, and then up a dozen dry mini-waterfalls up the first fork to the right from the beach before El Cabrito and then a thirty minute scramble up very steeply to the ridge above El Cabrito. You could try something similar, if being on the right track all the time bores you (you should take a companion with you for safety and a litre of water, and should allow 9 hours or more). If wanting to stay on the main suggested walk, pay particularly careful attention to the walk details just after the Barranco de Chinguarime, and be sure to head North for a substantial distance at this point (see the German map). It is also very easy on this walk to confuse a terrace for a path, and white arrows and white marks and mini-cairns for walk marks, when these may only be boundary markers.

The walk from Seima and El Cabrito onwards to San Sebastian has been improved by the authorities and no doubt the whole walk will be equally easy soon. The route has its own awesome majesty, and passes through very dilapidated terraces and through hamlets abandoned many years ago – it is hard to imagine that you are so close to two of the major towns on the island, and these lonely houses are bound to come to life soon, being so near to the new airport. Farmers in this part of the island used to rely on winter rains to fill their water reservoirs and to grow their barley. Even the superbly efficient Austrian community at El Cabrito, which uses liquids from its biological sewage plant to water the land, and has three pipes coming in from miles away with water from their reservoirs, had all these reservoirs completely dry when I visited, and was relying on its deep borehole.

Having got lost on two separate days, and having given up, simply making our own peculiar way through on this walk, the third time I was determined to find the orthodox route, and to do so walked it in the reverse direction from San Sebastian to Santiago. A force 9 gale was blowing. But it was my last possible day for walking, so I felt the need to persevere, my Chinese hat held on with both hands and my teeth, the hat acting as a sail and the wind throwing me around the mountain. Do not try some of the more precipitous walks on very windy days, it could be extremely dangerous. Luckily this walk is not one of narrow paths over high plunges. The pages were being ripped out of my notebook as I tried to note the path as if coming in the other direction, but I am confident that the details that follow are substantially correct.

The route out of Santiago as far as the beaches is described above in the section on Hippie Caves in Santiago. Carrying on from where those details left off: *You go up the 'Private Property Entry Forbidden' road* with its metal pipe barriers on each side of the road, your direction initially SE. This road becomes asphalted (with grass growing up the middle nevertheless) after 20 metres.

Near the top, the road forks three ways, and you go in the straight-on direction through two more metal pipe barriers on each side of the road, initially ESE/110 degrees – with a drystone wall to your left and an abandoned bulldozer ahead to your right. Keep on down towards the valley bottom of the next beach, **Playa de Chinguarime**. You follow the valley bottom along, on the left hand side of it. On the German map you are now heading up the **Barranco de Chinguarime** in a more or less Northerly direction. You come parallel to the alternative route down at the bottom of the barranco, coming up from the beach. Look across to your NE and you can see the continuation of your path, zigzagging up the hill, well to the right of the pylon on the horizon opposite.

Turn right at the end of the banana plantations, just past a workman's breeze block hut. You will have a high metal pillar fence on your left hand side. You are now on the German map's route 40. *The car road track goes round but you carry straight on to the mini-cairn ahead*, your direction initially Eastwards. *Now head up the zigzag path ahead*. It is a clear path. Within four minutes you pass a white post on your left. Hotel Tecina is soon visible back in Santiago. Towards the top follow the main path round to the left (you're heading initially for the pylon to your North, although your route will bend to the right some 150 metres short of it). You pass a drystone shelter 10 metres off your path to the right. Within 5 minutes, nearing the top, you may be able to spy in the distance the two tall palm trees of Casas de Contrera, several kilometres to your North, your interim destination (with the houses of Casas de Contrera above these palm trees).

Your path is well-defined, soon on a gentle gradient heading roughly North East.

Soon there is an outcrop of rock about 150 metres away to your North, and if you look carefully you will see the edge of a house on its right hand side (also to your North). This is the house you must in due course make for. It will turn out to be a drystone animal shelter and has three doorways, although the two doors on the right hand side are missing. Its tiled roof is intact.

Meanwhile, before your path turns steep left for this house, you should see ahead of you, on the other side of the barranco, a house to your East. Do not be tempted by the terrace that seems to lead towards it, as this is where we went wrong. Indeed if you reach the edge of the barranco which this house is on, a barranco which has a line of pylons on its far side, you have gone too far and need to retrace your steps some 100 metres or so. Visible above this house that misled us is the headland ridge above El Cabrito, on the furthest horizon, the far right sea end of which will, in some four hours' time, be your point of descent into El Cabrito.

When the crag with the three-door animal shelter becomes NNW of you (340 degrees), I have placed a mini-cairn to mark your 90 degree turn towards the crag, and there is another mini-cairn 15 metres up on your left. Your route is also up towards the line of the pylons, at 90 degrees to the line.

You come to the shelter and *your path is to the left of this house, just before the first side wall, and then behind it,* heading North. There is a faint red circle on the rock. You then continue, *heading under the pylon cables.* You are now within some 20 minutes from the top of the Chinguarime barranco (the one with the banana plantations). And shortly, for a while, *you will follow a mini-streambed,* later parallel and to the right hand side of it, on a path upwards. You are still at 90 degrees to the pylon cables.

At a mini-cairn, your path heads rightwards between terraces, your direction 80 degrees, and, within 40 metres, you see to your left ahead there is *a house,* which when you get closer to it, is distinctive – it has *a huge boulder forming part of its lower left wall,* and it has a threshing circle 20 metres in front of the houses, to the South.

Just past this threshing circle (and just before some more terraces begin) your path heads up (NNW/340 degrees). *You pass 15 metres below this house (which is on your left),* and you are within 12 minutes of the previous three door shelter.

You can now see the palm trees of Casas de Contrera more clearly to your North.

You pass on your right a drystone house with its tiled roof intact and short curved drystone wall extending from its seaward side.

The next house you come to, you pass below its wall, to its right, on the path between it and the barranco's side. (The house is drystone, with at the seaward end a tiled roof which is beginning to give way.)

Going up above the small barranco and the streambed below, *keep heading as always for the palm trees of Casas de Contrera to your North.*

Your path is well-defined and upwards at present. The streambed is below you to the right. *You cross at the streambed crossing, marked by mini-cairns on both sides.* I had a pleasant dip here one year when it was unusually deep.

Once across, there is a fork, with the right hand fork heading off, initially ESE/110 degrees, but you want the left hand fork, initially NNE/20 degrees, as you will be following up along the right hand side of the streambed for some way. There are mini-cairns marking the path.

You pass on your right the ruin of a drystone house that is still standing, a drystone shed and several more ruins.

You soon see on your right, to the other side of a small barranco, a number of houses, all still tiled except one, and a drystone kiln-shaped oven (your path does not go to these houses).

You go on the right hand side of a streambed towards a 'P+' painted white sign on a rock, your direction initially NNW/340 degrees. *35 metres past the P+ rock, you cross the streambed to your left,* the crossing marked by mini-cairns, going away from your destination, and *then head up it again,* keeping it this

76

time on your right.

Do not cross the streambed until the path makes this inevitable, when you are almost level with the palm trees. When it does cross the streambed, you continue your way up, the path marked by tiny cairns, towards the two palm trees above you (which are now to your NNE/20 degrees).

20 metres below the palm trees, a fork (initially Eastwards) goes off to your right in the direction of some houses, but *you want the path to the NNE/20 degrees, keeping to the left of the palms.*

When the first palm is about 15 metres away from you, your path goes uphill to the left, marked by a mini-cairn, in an initially WNW/290 degrees direction. (Don't be seduced by the glimpse of roof tiles and the white marks ahead of you.)

You pass the two palm trees on your right, and your upward path is towards the Casas de Contrera, currently hidden from sight some 500 metres away, with, leading to them, an upward zigzagging path over the right hand part of the summit above you. Look out for mini-cairns marking the way up.

You may come to the wooden cross next to and before Casas de Contrera (it may not still be there – it was nearly a gonner when I was there and would make a worthwhile restoration project.) From it you can see clearly to your East the headland ridge you will need above El Cabrito. Seima is however your next interim destination, to your NNE/20 degrees, and not yet visible. You must get there first before turning towards the sea.

The big two storey house in **Casas de Contrera** stores big wooden barrels and has one bed downstairs and two upstairs (one with rather a fine bedstead) and a wooden balcony with a rickety floor. It was pleasant to sit on the little chair in front of the house, eating my chocolate with some protection from the gale.

Facing the front of the house, a path comes in (to your WNW/290 degrees) beside the left hand side of the house. This is the path to Jerdune (German map routes 40 and 39). But *your onward path runs parallel to the front of the house,* some 25 metres way from it, in a direction that is initially WSW/260 degrees.

Leaving Casas de Contrera, *your path turns left by a drystone ruin with no roof,* which has a smaller shelter attached to its far end, your way initially North towards a mini-cairn on the right (and with two drystone shelters on the far skyline beyond).

Your path down is about 5 metres below a rock painted with 'A46' in white and the path is marked by a mini-cairn.

Then your path passes a rock painted with 'A47' on your left. Looking into the future, you can see your way up the other side of the barranco, a path snaking up to a mini-cairn on the skyline, to your ESE/110 degrees.

Once you actually cross the streambed, your onward path is unclear, but is marked by mini-cairns. By four trees enclosed in a drystone wall, turn right and follow the streambed to your left hand side for 25 metres, then cross over towards a mini-cairn – the first in 15 metres is to your SSE/160 degrees, then more heading 140 degrees. In 35 metres, you come to a boulder with green lichen on its top third and a mini-cairn on top of it. 100 metres on, heading East, you are nearing the edge of the next barranco, and *a T-junction of sorts. In front of you is a small amateurish drystone wall of red stones; here you go left on a defined path,* initially 30 degrees, passing a small drystone house with intact roof tiles some 35 metres below you on your right.

You go down over a streambed and up the other side on a clear path. At the top of the barranco, you can see some of the some 18 buildings of Seima ahead of you. Soon you go down over rocks, keeping slightly to your right.

Your immediate path is visible, if you look carefully, to your NNE/20 degrees, with a cairn on the next horizon to mark the way.

It is the upper group of houses in **Seima** that you are making for, not the lower terrace on the right (ie not the one which has the pre-eminently white house in it) and not the ones way up to the left with the palm trees. For your future orientation, note as you get closer the faded white house in the upper group that has a drystone wall extending from the right hand side of it – you will need to walk along under the wall, heading right, shortly.

From the top you descend into the tiny barranco barring you from Seima, following a gentle gradient down the left hand side of the valley (in the direction of the houses with the palm trees).

From the bottom, your way up is defined by small boulders along the side of the path which zigzags up. You come up towards a terrace of half a dozen houses (also to your SE) with tiled roofs more or less intact. The path heads left 90 degrees. *You pass on your right a large drystone house with a huge V-shaped gap for its front door, and no roof. Here you come to a T-junction and you turn right. The turn is marked by a mini-cairn.* Your path right is initially ESE/110 degrees.

You come to the substantial off-white ruined house complex, mentioned above, with part of its tiled roof remaining, but its five extensions have all lost theirs. The house is behind a 5 foot drystone wall on your left. From the far end of this wall, you can make out a further group of houses to head for, further on, quarter left, to your ESE/110 degrees.

You pass on your left an isolated drystone house, roofless, with its walls beginning to crumble. White rocks on the left hand side of the path mark your onward way. *Your direction is towards the large cairn in the distance*, now to your SE. From here to San Sebastian the path is much better defined (from El Cabrito it is a doddle).

Your path runs beneath a group of ruined houses (which have a drystone well in front of them). Your path is parallel to their front walls.

You come to the large cairn. You can make out from there the faint path you will need, way ahead on the left hand edge of the headland of El Cabrito to your ESE/110 degrees.

Within a couple of minutes of this large cairn, you may be able to see to your ESE/110 degrees (to the left of the slight crag ahead of you) a little nipple of stones sticking up. This is your interim destination.

Once on the fairly level ground along some terraces, you can see the beach before El Cabrito visible below you to your right/SSE/160 degrees. Ahead of you, to your East, you can see the wide beach of Playa de la Guancha. In between, El Cabrito beach lies hidden.

Soon you make your way diagonally down long-abandoned terraces. You pass the nipple, 20 metres to your left, and continue on, your direction 140 degrees, to the post with a sign for on it for the 'Monumento Natural Barranco del Cabrito'. Follow a well-defined path onwards.

Within 15 minutes, you pass under pylon cables. The path seems to peter out just before a mini-summit ahead of you. But just head on South over the centre of the mount with its slightly green rocks (a mini-cairn on its top). You will then pick up a couple of white arrows and a well-made path leading you down.

You follow the ridge – first the slightly brown earth path through the red rock ridge plateau. Ahead is your interim destination, a great cairn to your ESE/110 degrees, about a kilometre away, on the skyline above the ridge of the El Carbito barranco.

You come to a huge green-lichen-covered vertical knife edge of rock that forms part of the West side of the El Cabrito barranco – like a huge slice of toast pointing up. You go to the right of this – and you may see some white arrows marking your way.

Your onward path is not that clear, but head for another post with a sign on it for the Monumento Natural Barranco del Cabrito, to your SE. The path to this is red rock with an occasional chalky-white admixture.

From near the post, you can see your clear path down the right hand side of the barranco, to your ESE/110 degrees, into El Cabrito.

On the way down, a minor path heads down slightly to the right, but you stay on the main path to the left, initially NNE/20 degrees, *down towards the terrace of orange-tiled houses.*

About 200 metres above these houses, a way straight

on and initially upwards offers itself, but you turn right, down towards the beach, initially ESE/110 degrees.

El Cabrito is private property. They prefer only to give or sell you food or let you stay the night if in a dire emergency, and in such a case they may run a special boat trip for you for 5,000 pesetas. You can ask for water. Otherwise *they prefer you to keep to the right when you reach the orange-tiled houses and to take the long way round by heading for the boat pier on the right hand edge of the beach*. The pier is where you can perhaps catch their boat into San Sebastian. At Easter, El Cabrito tends to be packed full with 70 or so Austrian guests. Normally visitors come for two weeks, either for a holiday or for painting courses, with no way out by road, only by footpaths or by boat, and they pay from about 135 DM per day for complete board (children are looked after for the parents, and have a very full programme of their own).

From the boat pier, *you go along the beach to its far end, to the road left up the barranco*, in a NNW/340 degrees direction. You pass the dark rockface of the barranco side on the right, and *you come to five-pillared metal barrier on your right hand side (there is a netball post and shack with murals to your left hand side)*. Go through the middle of the barrier (it slides open) and your onward path has been made up to very high standards and is easy to follow, all the way in to San Sebastian.

Just in case: *Your route up is ahead of you, to the NNE/20 degrees, marked by a white marker 'P' and '65' on the rock below it*, and the solitary palm tree behind it (and the Monumento Natural sign to its right hand side). Straight on past mini-cairns, keep to the main track. Ignore a minor path to the right. Lift the barrier near the top (reached within 30 minutes of leaving the El Cabrito beach).

Go up to the large cairn on the bend and the Monumento Natural sign and head down (not the fork to your right, just before this; and straight on at the sign is route 38/39 to Bar Perraza). Head down to the **Playa de la Guancha** and avoid all forks off. On the final approach to the playa, keep on the left hand side of the streambed to pick up the onward path. The path fringes the beach. (The nicest part of the beach to swim, if the sun is still on it, is the Western end where there is a cove of rocks and sand.) There are four buildings on this beach and a goat shelter.

Your onward path up the next barranco is visible to your East, going diagonally up from left to right, to the top of the cliff above the sea. Keep to the main path, and to the same style of path, near the top (not taking the upper fork offered). Now your path is towards 'Mount Fuji' (El Teide on Tenerife). San Sebastian is ahead, and the figure of Jesus up on the mountain to your left. Your onward path is between Jesus and the sea, diagonally up from left to right.

You come to a T-junction. Turn right, and then immediately left down steps to the NW initially, so that your path will pass below Jesus. Ignore a right fork to a religious cross 20 metres away, turn left and continue down into town, with a fence on your right, with beyond it a gleaming industrial building and on into town.

Day 7

For those in Gomera for one week, who have followed the main suggested walks, the morning bus leaves from a few metres beyond the taxi rank in Hermigua towards San Sebastian (see bus times in the main Hermigua entry above; the moist reliable place to check bus times locally seems to be the Casa Creativa). It is wise to be at the bus stop earlier than the stated times. The bus goes all the way to the harbour in **San Sebastian**. You need to pick up a boarding card (tarjeta de embarque) there in the large port building (the right hand queue), even if you have a return hydrofoil ticket.

On the hydrofoil's arrival back in Los Cristianos, do not dilly-dally. We got stuck on the ship one year, and it took us over an hour to get off. We spent five minutes leisurely getting our things together after the boat docked, only to find that they had dispensed with the gangplank and were moving the boat out of the berth to another part of the port. Many 'tranquillo's and 'cinco minute' later, we discovered that most of the crew had gone over the side into lifeboats for a drill, and we had to persuade the captain to get half a dozen crew to manhandle an emergency gangway so that we could get to the airport.

A bus from the quayside departs on the ferry's arrival for Santa Cruz bus station.

Once, with time on our hands, we enjoyed the two-hour, 2,000-peseta boat trip offered in Los Cristianos to go out to see the Pilot whales, which grow up to 8 metres long. They swim to depths of 800 metres to eat the squid on which they rely, but they also seem happy to swim very close to the boats.

Bus stop for airport

To get to the airport bus stop (at the Playa de las Americas) from the port, you go away from the dock towards town, turn right round the back of the concrete fence behind which the small sailing boats are dry-docked, then less than halfway across the long beach, by the cluster of six palm trees, fork left ENE/70 degrees up the main shopping street, the Calle General Franco, alongside the cafes with awnings. Go up past the big white church, then straight on with the Pitaland to your left hand side. Turn right just past the taxi rank and the palatial Centro Cultural, both on your right hand side (just past the turning, if you miss it, there is the green cross symbol and ATN on your left hand side) and the next main road which crosses yours is the one with all the bus stops (you will see the Tropilana Cafe Bar on the other side of this main road, and you turn left and go to the Tropilana side of the road).

There are two stops for the No 487, the bus to the airport. You want the furthest away one, at the far upper end of the array of bus stops, with the Netto supermarket behind it. The stop's board is headed 'Aeropuerto del Sur'. On the board it gives as leaving times as 35 past each hour from 7.35am to 9.35pm (although the 2.35pm bus does not run on Saturdays, Sundays or festival days).

Male schoolkids once tried to force their way to the front when the 2.35pm bus arrives, so if you need to catch the plane and the bus looks likely to fill up, you may have to be forceful yourself in resisting queue-jumpers.

Day 7 Alternative: Bar Peraza to La Laja and Lomo Fragoso or Rock Agando

Toughness: 5. Beauty: 6. Hours: 5.

If you have spare time in Gomera on Day 7, a pleasant and easy short walk is to get a lift, bus or a taxi to Bar Peraza and there take the route 33 to La Laja, and then either back up to complete the circle, via Rock Agando, or on down from La Laja to Lomo Fragoso (I have swum in the icy pools down below the road here. Streams from these pools feed into the reservoirs).

The way down to La Laja is excessively well signposted and takes about 1 hour and 15 minutes; it is a stroll from there down to Lomo Fragoso (another hour and a half at most). There you can catch a lift or phone for a taxi (tel San Sebastian 922 870524 – there is a bar in Lomo Fragoso) or continue walking – as the exigencies of your schedule or purse may dictate. Beware that there is little traffic on this road for hitching, however.

From La Laja coming back up to Bar Peraza via Rock Agando (the Northern branch of route 33) means a total circular tour of up to three and a half hours – perhaps allow four hours if you have a ferry to catch (it took me only three hours, even with my notes to write). As a result of the walk being rather boringly over-developed for tourists, I find the climb up to Rock Agando rather arduous, more tiring psychologically than springing like a goat up and down barrancos, with the risk of getting lost keeping me alert. However, at the top there is a rewarding walk along a more level stretch to the Ermita de las Nieves, which, if earned by the previous uphill climb, always feels to me like a lovely way to say goodbye to Gomera.

You can hardly get lost once underway: Most of the route is marked by little yellow double triangles with the image of a walking person within them, plus by occasional huge drystone towers with incongruous signposts sticking out of them.

The details for the walk are as follows: *As if coming out of the* **Bar Peraza***, turn left uphill on the main asphalt road. Within 150 metres you come to the viewing platform on your right (called Degollada de Peraza). On the right hand side of this platform is a wide stone path down*, with occasional steps, initially heading North, across a thin waterpipe.

The main village of Lomo Fragoso is immediately visible below you to the NE, and a part of La Laja, your interim destination, is visible to your NNW/340 degrees – as is your onward path towards it.

You keep to the main path ignoring all turn-offs. Within 20 minutes, you come to the first drystone tower saying that La Laja is onwards, and that Degollada de Peraza is behind you.

Within 30 minutes of starting out, you turn a corner and have a clear view of La Laja strung out below you, with pear-shaped Rock Agando to your WNW/290 degrees. I could already hear voices from La Laja, although it was more than a kilometre away.

About 100 metres from the first houses in **La Laja***, ignore a turn-off to the left.* You then come to a drystone tower with three ways indicated, at which point you either go straight on down to La Laja and Lomo Fragoso, if you have so decided – in which case your route needs no further explanation – or upwards to Rock Agando (initially NNW/340 degrees). Taking this route, you soon come to yellow triangles/man walking signs on your left.

Within 10 minutes of starting back up you pass a newly retiled drystone house and outhouse.

Then within 15 minutes of this start, you come to a triple-way drystone tower, with its middle sign (to La Laja) broken. You want the left hand way that continues upwards to Rock Agando, initially Westwards.

You are soon passing the last houses of La Laja and it is grindingly steep. Keep to the main path. Within 35 minutes of starting to climb, you pass a huge drystone wire-netted water barrier wall on your right, and within a further 5 minutes another one, and within a further 5 minutes, a third one.

You go over a little wooden plank bridge, under a large eucalyptus tree, and shortly two more such bridges.

Then comes the last of the wire-netted water barriers.

And so you come to a drystone house on the right, with a roofed and pillared colonnade extension at the front. This is a hut for travellers, I believe, marked **Degollade del Tanque** on the German map, and certainly there were two German youths trying to set up a tent outside in the high wind when I was there. You are now within an hour of starting upwards, and within half an hour at most of reaching the asphalt road above.

Round the corner from the hut you can see the parapet of the main road still a disheartening height above you (to your SSW/200 degrees).

You pass a peak on your right, Rock Ojila (1170 metres) which is like a carbon copy of its higher neighbour, Rock Agando (1250 metres).

Soon you encounter drystone-style steps, but mortared. And after two more encounters with such steps, *you are back on the main road*, within about one and a half hours of starting your climb. (The sign at the exit, in case you are coming the other way, says 'Parque Nacional Garajonay' and is about 100 metres down the asphalt road from Rock Agando. Its direction is initially NE, down drystone-style mortared steps, with an earth path continuation clearly visible.)

If in a hurry, you can hitch leftwards from here to San Sebastian, but if you have time, savour the final short path to the Ermita de las Nieves. For this you *head up the main road to the left for 300 metres* past crash barriers on both sides of the road, and *opposite a rock fall road sign on the right of the road, there is a path going steeply upwards to the left*, its direction initially SSE/160 degrees. Take it.

Within a couple of minutes you are going up a rocky unclear path, whose general direction (SE) is nevertheless clear.

Then it is a level enough stroll still just within sight of the road, until the path becomes more rocky and leads further away from the main road. For a spell downwards, the path is shaded by heather-like trees. And it soon joins a car track, with the Ermita's terrace wall, and the trees screening the Ermita, visible ahead of you to your ESE/110 degrees. You are within 13 minutes of starting up from the main road.

The **Ermita de las Nieves** has picnic tables and a row of stone basins with working taps.

You go past the Ermita onto its far terrace, and your continuation path is off to the left, initially ENE/70 degrees, parallel to the car track below, and heading towards your destination, the Bar Peraza, below the large red and white TV aerial to your East.

Your trail, parallel to the car track, soon peters out down into the car track. Carry on down this, parallel to the asphalt road below.

Take the next fork left, 50 metres past 'A/A' painted in white on a rock to your left, up a red earth car track to your left, heading up initially ESE/110 degrees, and leaving the main car track that continues on.

On top you can see the large red and white TV aerial ahead of you to your right. *Keep on upwards, ignoring a clear fork to the left.*

You go on down past another smaller red and white aerial with a hut and solar panels beneath it. You head down between green fences, going straight on towards the larger more distant aerial, and staying on this track, which within 5 minutes of the small aerial, narrows down and has a metal fence on its right. You go downwards on a rocky path, Bar Peraza a mere 400 metres ahead of you. *It is a final 50 metres of very sharp descent indeed* (but there are rocky steps) down to the asphalt road.

(If coming up the other way, this steep path up is marked with a green and red dot, and leads up, initially WNW/290 degrees. It is 15 metres below a right hand bend road sign, it is 10 metres above a road sign saying 'Arure 21, Valle Gran Rey 34 and TF 713', and it is 20 metres above a sharp fork off right to Santiago, and 30 metres above La Degollada de Peraza.)

From there it's a short walk downhill to the **Bar Peraza** on your right, from which you can hitch or take a taxi (tel San Sebastian 922 870524) back into San Sebastian (or find your way down along the German map's route 37, if you have time to explore this trail).

Two weeks on Gomera

There are two weeks' worth of walks in this guide. For those planning a second week of walking, my suggestion would be to make a second and different circuit of the island. My Day 6 main walk ends in Hermigua. From here get a bus or a lift or a taxi to Vallehermoso for the night.

• Day 8: The beautiful Day 3 Alternative walk will bring you to Las Hayas and Bar Montana. From here take the Day 3 Alternative down into Valle Gran Rey.

• Day 9: Spend the inevitable day on the beach and in Valle Gran Rey.

• Day 10: Climb back out of the valley to Chipude.

• Day 11: And from there do either the walk from Chipude to Pajarito, via the summit of Garajonay and then hitch to Alajero, or the alternative short Day 4 half-day walk from Chipude to Alajero.

• Day 12: From Alajero there is then the delightful Day 5 Alternative walk via Benchijigua to Santiago.

• Day 13: You could end with the awesome Day 7 Alternative Santiago to San Sebastian walk.

• Day 14: Any more walking time before your departure could be spent on the Day 7 walk from Bar Peraza to Lomo Fragoso, or on whichever walk you didn't do on Day 11.

• Day 15, onwards: By now you are a veteran, and can probably find your way using just the German map, the compass and questions to locals and other walkers, plus allowing time for getting lost.

Notes for your updates and corrections:

Please send your detailed updates and corrections – and say which edition you are correcting (this is the 6th) – to Nicholas Albery, Alternative Gomera, 20 Heber Road, London NW2 6AA (tel 020 8208 2853; fax 020 8452 6434; rhino@dial.pipex.com; www.gomera.org.uk). You will be helping your fellow travellers and will be credited in the update sheets and will be sent a copy. Updates can also be accessed online.

Main Institute for Social Inventions publications

• **Alternative Gomera**, by Nicholas Albery. 6th edition, £9-99. Map £5-85. Both including p&p.

• **Time Out Book of Country Walks – 52 walks within easy reach of London**, edited by Nicholas Albery, assisted by Hugh Kelly. Walks are reached by train, and each has a pub at lunch and a tea place. Includes free membership of the self-organising Saturday Walkers' Club. £10-99 including p&p.

• **Social Dreams & Technological Nightmares – A global ideas bank compendium**, predicting the next 500 years, £14-85 incl. p&p.

• **Creative Speculations**, 'an amazing book, ambitious and successful' (Stewart Brand). £14-85 incl. p&p.

• The above two books, plus **DIY Futures** (£14-85 on its own) are available as a special package for £35-85 (inc p&p) *if ordered by a new Institute subscriber.*

• **The Forest Garden** by Robert Hart. How to establish a minimal-labour Forest Garden, in town or country, consisting entirely of fruit and nut trees and bushes, wild and self-seeding vegetables and herbs; with the story of Hart's own Shropshire Forest Garden & diet. £3-25. 3rd edition.

• **The New Natural Death Handbook**, 3rd edition. Cheap, Green and DIY funerals, 120 plus woodland burial grounds, cardbaord coffins, Good Funeral Guide to undertakers, caring for the dying at home, preparing for dying, living wills. £12-99 (£13-50 1st class).

• **Poem for the Day – 366 Poems, Old and New, Worth Learning by Heart**, with foreword by Wendy Cope. 400 page book with a poem for each day of the year – and an associated Poetry Challenge. £11-49.

• **1,001 Health Tips** – from recent medical research. Get well and stay well, the ways that work, beneficial for all ages, guaranteed to surprise and inform. £6-85. FREE! to new Institute susbscribers.

• **The Neal's Yard Story**, how an extraordinary oasis of greenery and green businesses has created over 100 jobs on the edge of Covent Garden; full of useful ideas for small businesses and urban renewal. £1-95.

• The book **Community Counselling Circles**, how to apply a new method for improving the atmosphere in groups, illustrated with over 260 diagrams. £6-95; libraries etc. £9-95.

• **The Solution for South Africa**, the brilliant and influential cantonisation scheme backed by the Groundswell movement, £7.

• **Being True to Yourself**, by Margaret Chisman. These exercises for groups encourage insight and self-undertanding. £4-95.

• **Auction of Promises - how to raise £16,000 in one evening**, by Kara Conti, for church, school and community groups. How to auction off services such as 4 hours' massage, computer consultancy etc. £1-95.

• The Institute **Journal**. Subscriptions £15 per annum (£17 by credit card from abroad). Subscribers receive at least one annual bumper book each year, plus '1,001 Health Tips', plus 10% off many publications and other benefits.

Payment by credit card (Visa or Mastercard only): This is the cheapest way to pay from abroad.

Add 9 per cent for European airmail and 32 per cent for foreign airmail.

Cheques etc to: **The Institute for Social Inventions**, 20 Heber Road, London NW2 6AA, UK (tel 020 8208 2853; fax 020 8452 6434; e-mail: rhino @dial.pipex.com).

Orders may also be paid securely online by credit card at www.globalideasbank. org/bookorder.html

Institute-launched websites include:
• Alternative Gomera (www.gomera.org.uk)
• The Global Ideas Bank (www.globalideasbank.org)
• ApprenticeMaster Alliance (www.apprentice.org.uk)
• Natural Death Centre (www.naturaldeath.org.uk)
• Participatory events in every city in the world (www.DoBe.org)
• Time Out Saturday Walkers Club (www.walking club.org.uk)